A SOCIAL AND POLITICAL HISTORY OF THE MEXICAN-AMERICAN POPULATION OF TEXAS, 1929-1963

by

Robert A. Cuellar

Thesis

State University

1969

REPRINTED IN 1974 BY

    R AND E RESEARCH ASSOCIATES
    4843 MISSION ST., SAN FRANCISCO 94112
    18581 McFARLAND AVE., SARATOGA, CA 95070

PUBLISHERS AND DISTRIBUTORS OF ETHNIC STUDIES

    EDITOR: ADAM S. ETEROVICH
    PUBLISHER: ROBERT D. REED

LIBRARY OF CONGRESS CARD CATALOG NUMBER

74-76565

ISBN

0-88247-245-3

TABLE OF CONTENTS

LIST OF ILLUSTRATIONS

INTRODUCTION

The study of any ethnic group in the United States should begin with a suitable expression accurately denoting the parental background of the people concerned. Acute sensitivity of the group, when aggravated by a misnomer, compounds the problem. In writing about the social and political history of Americans of Mexican descent from 1929 to 1963, one must consciously refer to that group with a strong emphasis on their national loyalty, yet hyphenate their name with a reference to their descriptive identification. An example of the difficulty of finding a suitable expression is mentioned by Carey McWilliams, editor of the national newsmagazine, The Nation, who suggested the generally accepted phrase "Spanish-speaking," but at the same time found such a term too extensive, since it included Americans whose Spanish-speaking background could be traced to other countries besides Mexico.[1]

The phraseology used in twentieth century magazines and newspapers to refer to United States citizens of Mexican parentage has contributed to this difficulty. Most writers simply used the expression "Mexican," a term which has become unacceptable to most members of this ethnic group, not on the basis of nationality, but on the assumption of racial difference. Leaders within the Spanish-speaking group have stated that a citizen of the United States, by birth or naturalization, should not be identified as a foreigner merely because his forefathers migrated to the United States from a different country. The Spanish-speaking Texan, therefore, can not be a Mexican if the only link he has with Mexico is his ancestral background.[2]

Any phrase used to characterize members of the Spanish-speaking population is to some extent misleading, inaccurate, and at times offending. In order not to detract from the Mexican culture of Americans with such background, and to avoid the resentment created by the erroneous term "Mexican," it is necessary to resort to the hypenated expression "Mexican-American."[3]

It is equally as difficult to find fitting terminology to refer to Texans whose parentage is other than Mexican, Indian, Oriental, or Negro as it is to find one for Mexican-Americans. Spanish-speaking Americans have used the term "Anglo-American" to refer to any citizen who is not a member of any group mentioned above.[4] Throughout this study the most widely accepted terms, Mexican-American and Anglo-American, will be used although other expressions will appear periodically to avoid excessive repetition.

FOOTNOTES

[1] Carey McWilliams, North From Mexico: The Spanish-speaking People of the United States (New York, 1948), p. 7.

[2] Walter Fogel, Education and Incomes of Mexican-Americans in the Southwest (Los Angeles, 1965), pp. V-VI.

[3] Ibid., p. 43.

[4] Ibid., p. 8; U.S. Congress, House of Representatives, "Representative Gonzalez speaking about Poverty and Discrimination in the Southwest," 89th Cong., 2nd Sess., May 12, 1966, Congressional Record, CXII, 10479.

CHAPTER I

HISTORICAL BACKGROUND OF THE MEXICAN-AMERICAN

MOVEMENT TOWARDS SOCIAL INVOLVEMENT

IN TEXAS

The Spanish-speaking population of Texas, numbering approximately 1,500,000, comprises one of the largest ethnic groups in the state. To get a clear understanding of the geographical area of the state in which the majority of Mexican-Americans reside, an imaginary line can be drawn diagonally from El Paso to San Antonio and from San Antonio to Corpus Christi. Between this line and the Texas-Mexico boundary is the majority of the Spanish-speaking population of Texas. In recent years the metropolitan areas such as Houston, Dallas, and Fort Worth have attracted a large number of Texans of Mexican descent seeking the employment opportunities lacking in the rural areas of south Texas.[1] Their concentration in the southern half of the state, however, remains so heavy that the number of Spanish-speaking Texans living in Hidalgo, Cameron, Nueces, Harris, Webb, and Bexar counties account for a large portion of the entire Mexican-American citizenry of Texas.[2]

The history of the Mexican-American population dates back to the early sixteenth century, when the Spanish conquistadores subdued the Aztec Indians at Tenochtitlan, now Mexico City. The absence of Spanish women resulted in intermarriage between the Spanish soldiers and Indian women and the development of a new culture which became socially subordinate to the "pure blooded" Spaniard. This mixed race of Spanish and Indian parentage increased numerically as more Indian tribes were vanquished by the militarily and culturally superior Europeans and as more Spaniards ventured from the old to the new world.[3]

In the late seventeenth century the Spaniards began settling the region of present-day Texas. A large number of the pioneers were mestizos, the Spanish-Indian offspring, who settled and remained in this area until after the 1836 Texas revolution, when Texans declared their independence from Mexico to form a sovereign republic. During the decade that followed Texas's independence, Mexican immigrants crossed the Rio Grande and settled in the disputed area between the Nueces River and the Rio Grande.[4]

As a result of the Mexican-American War which lasted from 1846 to 1848, and the Treaty of Guadalupe Hidalgo that marked the end of the struggle, the United States acquired from the defeated nation a vast portion of territory extending from Texas to the Pacific coast of California and north to the forty-second parallel and the Arkansas River. According to the terms of the treaty, the government of the United States granted American citizenship to the Mexican residents of the ceded territory. This newly acquired citizenry, enhanced by normal population growth and immigration from Mexico, eventually became one of the largest ethnic groups in Texas and the United States. By 1880, for example, the Mexican population concentrated in the Texas territory south of the Nueces River amounted to approximately 50,000.[5]

The extensive surge of the Spanish-speaking population of Texas did not occur, however, until the early part of the twentieth century when, in 1911, the people of Mexico revolted against the dictator Porfirio Diaz who had firmly controlled the country for thirty-five years. La Revolucion disrupted the family life of most Mexicans and thousands migrated to the United States to escape the rigors touched off by the struggle. Many Mexican refugees never returned to their homeland but established themselves permanently in Texas and other areas of the Southwest where a large number of Mexican-Americans lived already. Upon their arrival to Texas, the Mexican immigrants, attracted by similarities in language, customs, and religion, settled in communities where other newly-arrived Mexicans and Spanish-speaking Texans resided. This isolation of the newcomers from the Anglo-American citizens evolved into the well-known barrios of today, run-down neighborhoods where the residents are predominantly Spanish-speaking, and are a part of practically every town where a sizable Mexican-American population is concentrated.[6]

The existing cultural differences and the lack of social contact of the two groups of Texans, coupled with the proximity of Mexico to Texas, prevented the Americanization of the Texans of Mexican ancestry. This segregation was clearly detrimental to the political cultivation of the Spanish-speaking Americans, who for generations remained alien to the political process in the United States. Their lack of understanding of American institutions led to nonparticipation in civic and governmental affairs in their communities and state.[7]

The Texans of Mexican descent, unmindful of civic and political matters, became primarily concerned with earning a living. Their opportunities, however, were limited to employment in the fields or as domestic servants. As The Texas Observer, a liberally-oriented Texas journal, pointed out in tracing the history of the Mexican-Americans of Texas:

> The Mexicans in America have done the dirty work of the Southwest. They built railroads, they planted and harvested the crops, here and elsewhere as migrants. They washed the dishes and cooked the food and kept the houses and cut the grass, and they still do these things.[8]

The status of the Mexican-American as cheap labor was passed on from father to son until the entire Spanish-speaking population in the United States became identified as migrants traveling, year after year, to East Texas and other parts of the country to harvest the crops. In 1940 an estimated 400,000 transient workers, two-thirds of whom were Mexican-Americans, earned their subsistence by going from one cotton-producing region to the next. This population, usually propertyless and with little or no education, found itself without the opportunity to participate in the social and political life of the state.[9]

The social inequality of the Mexican-American and Anglo-American groups created suspicion and distrust which further prevented a close relationship between the two peoples. Some Anglo-American citizens regarded their Spanish-speaking fellow-Texans as ". . . lazy, shiftless, jealous, cowardly, bigoted, superstitious, backward, and immoral," while a portion of the Mexican-Americans accused their opposites of being, ". . . arrogant, overbearing, aggressive, conniving, rude, unreliable, and dishonest."[10] Reconciliation of the two cultures, with these misunderstandings between them, was difficult to bring about. Above all, the resentment still prevails among many Mexican-American leaders who know that the political indifference of their people is, in part, the result of the traditional system of peonage which led to the emergence of political bossism.[11]

The attempts of Texas-Mexican leaders to change the Spanish-speaking population's ignorance and apathy into a conscious awareness of their civic responsibilities began in the early 1920's with the formation of the first Mexican-American civic and cultural club. These spokesmen, through such an organization, aimed to use the more advanced elements of their people to teach their masses about the process of democratic government. In addition, the initiators of the Mexican-American group planned for more subtle progress for citizens of Mexican descent by assimilating this ethnic group into the social and economic mainstream of Texas life. They also hoped to eliminate much of the discrimination and misunderstanding prevalent between the Anglo-Americans and their fellow-Texans of Mexican ancestry.[12]

The movement to organize the Mexican-American population into groups designed for its social advancement did not develop as a steady, uninterrupted awakening of a passive and indifferent group of Texans. It advanced sporadically through inspiration caused by the two world wars where many young soldiers with Mexican backgrounds first learned to have equality with the Anglo-Americans.

Once this ethnic group achieved social acceptance the Spanish-speaking leaders sought direct participation in the political affairs of the state. It must be understood that Mexican-American politics meant anything from the extinction of political bossism or social discrimination to electing a city councilman or a governor. In tracing the history of the Texas population of Mexican descent the parallelism of the awakening of this group of people to social and cultural customs of Texas and their educational economic and political progress will become apparent.

FOOTNOTES

CHAPTER I

[1]Walter Moore, editor, <u>Texas Almanac and State Industrial Guide, 1968-69</u> (Dallas, 1967), p. 168.

[2]Carey McWilliams, <u>North From Mexico: The Spanish-speaking People of the United States</u> (New York, 1948), p. 48.

[3]Ibid., p. 85.

[4]Hubert H. Bancroft, <u>History of the North Mexican States and Texas,</u> Vol. XV of <u>The Works of Hubert Howe Bancroft,</u> 39 vols. (San Francisco, 1884), pp. 399-406.

[5]McWilliams, op.cit., p. 85; <u>The Texas Observer,</u> December 9, 1966, pp. 3-4; Raul Morin, <u>Among the Valiant: Mexican-Americans in WWII</u> and Korea (Los Angeles, 1963), p. 18.

[6]Morin, op.cit., pp. 18-19.

[7]Ibid., p. 19.

[8]<u>The Texas Observer</u>, December 9, 1966, p. 3.

[9]James W. Vander Zander, <u>American Minority Relations</u> (New York, 1966), p. 249.

[10]McWilliams, op. cit., p.99.

[11]Ibid., p. 86.

[12]O. Douglas Weeks, "The League of United Latin-American Citizens: A Texas-Mexican Civic Organization," <u>The Southwestern Political and Social Science</u> Quarterly, X (December, 1929), 264-67.

CHAPTER II

THE LEAGUE OF UNITED LATIN-AMERICAN CITIZENS:

FIRST MEXICAN-AMERICAN EFFORT TOWARDS

SOCIAL PARTICIPATION

During the 1920's the American citizen of Mexican descent in Texas found himself in a disadvantaged social position. Regarded by some of the majority ethnic leadership as a second-class citizen, he was constantly the victim of social prejudices. The opportunities for an accelerated assimilation into the American society were curtailed when both groups, the Anglo-American and Mexican-American, failed to cross the social boundary lines and kept isolated from one another. The social conditions of the Spanish-speaking population became worse, owing to the heavy immigration of Mexican citizens to the United States during this period. The new arrivals, unlettered in English and generally unskilled, worked in the cotton and vegetable fields alongside of and sometimes in competition with the United States citizen of Mexican descent. [1]

The Mexican-American population, constituting the lower stratum of society in Texas, was primarily preoccupied with earning a living; therefore, any other phase of life became secondary or unimportant. As a result of his economic impoverishment, the citizen of Mexican descent did not take part in state political action. This isolation led to apathy and indifference towards the governmental conditions that surrounded the predominantly Spanish-speaking communities. The extent of civic participation of the average Mexican-American citizen amounted to casting his ballot according to the instructions of his political patron. [2]

Among the Spanish-speaking citizenry of Texas lived a small but significant portion of families who enjoyed some degree of education, social status, and economic independence. These families, concentrated in the border towns such as Brownsville, Rio Grande City, Laredo, and El Paso, became apprehensive of the conditions under which their more unfortunate fellow-Texans were compelled to live. These middle class Americans were concerned with inequities such as the United States Census Bureau's classification of all persons of Mexican descent, whether American citizens or Mexican aliens, as "Mexicans" to distinguish them from the "white" population. These same community leaders worried about persons of Mexican backgrounds who had become so politically apathetic that they remained lackadaisical in their role as a part of Texas's democratic process.[3]

These Texans--doctors, lawyers, teachers, and businessmen--regarded themselves members of the American middle class and yearned to reverse the trend of political, economic, and social exploitation of their fellow Mexican-Americans. In an effort to change the traditional practice of a political "boss" who used the vote of the citizen of Mexican descent to his personal gains, the reform-minded leaders hoped for a new climate in the attitude of politicians who tended to take the Mexican-American ballot for granted. Many of the majority-supported power brokers failed to concern themselves with the problems of their Spanish-speaking constituents. This particular ethnic group needed, according to their new leaders, responsible spokesmen who understood the needs of all citizens. They concluded, therefore, that the solution was in teaching the population of Mexican background citizenship responsibility, and the value of the ballot as a tool to choose political representatives resonsive to their needs.[4]

A Mexican-American citizenry well educated in social and governmental affairs, the desired goal of most Spanish-speaking leaders, could only be created by an effectively organized group with a prolific plan for accomplishments. Such a need for organization was recognized, not to promote opposition to the Anglo-American residents, but to eliminate existing prejudices and inequities through the enhancement of social and political participation of the Mexican-American citizenry. Once effective unity became a reality, the leaders of this ethnic group believed, the American of Mexican descent could have political power, which, if properly guide, would secure solutions to other key-priority problems such as illiteracy, poverty, and social improvement.[5]

The yearnings and aspirations of the Texans of Mexican background--to better
the lot of their fellow-Americans--became apparent during the early 1920's in the form
of fraternal organizations for the purpose of striving towards a common goal. The first
such group was organized in San Antonio, Texas, in 1921. The constitution of this newly
formed group, The Order of the Sons of America (La Orden Hijos de America), restricted
its memberships exclusively to citizens of the United States of Mexican or Spanish descent, either native or naturalized. Although The Order of the Sons of American claimed
to be non-political, it encouraged Mexican-Americans to ". . . use their influence in all
fields of social, economic and political action in order to realize the greatest enjoyment
possible of all the rights and privileges and prerogatives extended by the American Constitution. . . ."[6]

The success of The Order of the Sons of America, although locally effective, was
short-lived. Its ambition to become national in scope never materialized, as only seven
groups were formed in South Texas. The work of this organization was not in vain, for
it laid the groundwork for future movements and led to the formation of other groups.[7]

On August 24, 1927, several Mexican-American leaders from Harlingen launched
a more effective and representative group than the one operating in San Antonio when
they called upon interested persons, including representatives of The Order of the Sons
of America, to unite into a strong society that would work for the needs of the Spanish-
speaking Texans. The emerged group, The League of Latin-American Citizens,[8]
adopted a constitution and organizational structure similar to the previously organized
association--The Order of the Sons of America. The League of Latin-American Citizens
moved swiftly, and within a short period of time groups were established at Brownsville,
McAllen, Grulla, Encino, and Laredo.[9]

The lack of success of the newly organized civic league disappointed the more
impatient and radical reformers, who demanded better unity and a more rapid pace of
organization. On February 17, 1929, in consequence of that attitude, three groups of
Spanish-speaking leaders met at Corpus Christi, Texas, to merge into a group with the
common objective of Mexican-American advancement. The clubs represented there
were the Corpus Christi Council of The Order of the Sons of America, The League of

Latin-American Citizens, and The Order of the Knights of America of San Antonio.[10]
The assemblage chose for its name The League of United Latin-American Citizens, and
called for a constitutional convention to take place at Corpus Christi on May 19, 1929.[11]

Meeting on schedule, the delegates drew up a constitution and completed the framework for formal organization.[12] The second article of the constitution clearly stated that
The League would be non-political, that its aims and purposes would be the eradication
of discriminatory practices based on race, religion, or social position. It also called
for the election of public figures ". . . who show, by their deeds, respect and consideration for our people," and for the equal representation and participation of the Mexican-American people on juries and in the administration of governmental affairs.[13] The
overriding objective in this plan of union seemed to be the social and political solidification of this ethnic group.

Instantaneous success greeted the efforts of The League in its first year of existence when followers organized eighteen lodges throughout the south and southwestern
parts of Texas. By 1934 the number of local groups grew to forty-three. In order to
provide for further expansion and growth The League designated the Supreme Council,
a group consisting of the highest officials in the organization, as the final authority in
matters of legislation and policy.[14]

LULAC's search for improved political and social conditions for the Spanish-speaking citizenry was the first real effort put forth by any segment of this ethnic group
to unite successfully for the purpose of voicing its needs and aspirations. The League
encountered massive problems that affected the citizens of Mexican descent which had
long been in existence and, therefore, difficult to solve. In spite of adverse experiences,
the new voice for this group of Texans gained initial success in securing educational facilities for previously neglected children, and brought about integration in some public
schools. In addition, The League's leaders established adult night schools in various
communities ". . . to teach the English language, and to train for citizenship and
worthy home membership."[15]

The men heading LULAC, although educated to some extent and highly motivated,
had little experience in civic functions; consequently, they found the task of Americanizing

the Spanish-speaking population too comprehensive for rapid progress. These Mexican-American reformers, aware of their own shortcomings, pioneered for a better educated youth to play dominant roles in the organization. With this purpose in mind, the hierarchy of The League favored a selective system of recruiting the membership for their group. They decided, after some discussion, to accept only the most advanced elements of the Spanish-speaking population in order to guide the less fortunate and to prevent the organizations from falling prey to the designs of politicians who could easily take advantage of a diluted group made up of members with limited educational attainments. [16]

As a non-political organization The League sought, and continues to seek, an "education for effective citizenship and not a Sophist's training in the tricks of practical politics. . . ." The leaders of this group, steering clear of direct involvement in governmental affairs, recognized the importance of the ballot as the weapon which politicians understood best. It became essential, therefore, to work towards making the Mexican-American citizen aware of his democratic privileges and to encourage every qualified voter to exercise this prerogative. [17]

With The League's success in eliminating the most obvious discriminatory practices throughout the state the dreams held by many reform-minded Spanish-speaking citizens for better living conditions began to turn into reality. Mexican-Americans, as a consequence of their new hopes, became interested in civic affairs and enthusiastically participated in poll tax paying campaigns and other functions to qualify and to induce other members of this group to participate in elections.

The increase in the number of Spanish-speaking voters, a result of the efforts of LULAC, did not change the indifferent attitude of politicians who sustained the loyalty of their constituents by using political bassism. The governmental influence of the citizenry of Mexican descent continued to be insignificant, in part owing to the apathy of members of this ethnic group towards civic affairs and their clannishness, which contributed to make assimilation difficult. [18]

The activities of The League as the first significant Spanish-speaking organization were many and its success was impressive, especially in the fields of education and the elimination of discriminatory practices throughout South Texas. The conservatism of the group's members and leaders, their lack of experience in organized work, and the challenge posed by such a comprehensive social problem as the plight of the Mexican-American citizenry prevented The League from making revolutionary changes in the social status of the Americans of Mexican descent. In Article 1, Section 3, of The League's constitution, the founders advised their membership to "Be proud of your origin and maintain it immaculate, respect your glorious past and help defend the rights of all the people."[19]

During the 1920's and 1930's the Spanish-speaking population of Texas needed to break away from its past, contrary to the advice of the early reformers, and make a bold leap towards a more progressive future. The Mexican-American, in preparation for a more effective role in the political arena of the state, needed a more radical program of education and indoctrination in the democratic system of government. Although The League failed to revolutionize the progress of the American of Mexican descent, it effectively accelerated the Americanization of this ethnic group of people whose attitude had deteriorated to a point of almost complete social and political apathy and economic resignation.

From the time of LULAC's organization in 1929 to the conclusion of the Second World War in 1945, The League remained partially active. The group, in a slow-moving, almost evolutionary, pace solved many local and state social problems of the Mexican-American population, but many of this group's ills remained unchanged. The persistent social afflictions eventually led to the formation of groups with more forceful demands. The creation of more progressive groups, in turn, caused The League of United Latin-American Citizens to regain some of its lost momentum in the fight for social and political equality for Americans of Mexican descent, but not before a new social group appeared on the Texas scene.

FOOTNOTES

CHAPTER II

[1]Paul Schuster Taylor, <u>An American-Mexican Frontier, Nueces County, Texas</u> (Chapel Hill, North Carolina, 1934), pp. 100-101.

[2] George I. Sanchez, "The American of Mexican Descent," The Chicago Jewish Forum, XX (Winter, 1961-62), 120-24.

[3] Ibid.

[4] Taylor, An American-Mexican Frontier, pp. 91-92; O. Douglas Weeks, "The League of United Latin-American Citizens: A Texas-Mexican Civic Organization," The Southwestern Political and Social Quarterly, X (December, 1929), 258-59.

[5] O. Douglas Weeks, op.cit., 258-59.

[6] Ibid., p. 260.

[7] Ibid.,

[8] This group, organized in 1927, is not to be confused with The League of United Latin-American Citizens which was formed in 1929 and is still in existence today.

[9] Weeks, op.cit., pp. 261-62.

[10] The Order of the Knights of America of San Antonio was originally a member group of The Order of the Sons of America, but seceded shortly after the former's organization and adopted the new name.

[11] Weeks, op.cit., pp. 262-63; Carey McWilliams, North from Mexico: The Spanish-speaking People of the United States (New York, 1948), p. 88. McWilliams cites Harlingen as the place and 1929 as the year of The League of United Latin-American Citizen's initial organization. He probably confused this group with the League initiated in 1927.

[12] The League of United Latin-American Citizens will be cited hereafter as "The League" or "LULAC."

[13] The League of United Latin-American Citizens, The Constitution and By-Laws of The League of United Latin-American Citizens, unpublished document, Austin, Texas, 1955, pp. 1-3, located in the office of the executive secretary of LULAC, Houston, Texas.

[14] Taylor, op.cit., p. 242; Weeks, op.cit., pp. 266-67.

[15] Edward D. Garza, "LULAC (League of United Latin-American Citizens)," unpublished master's thesis, Department of History, Southwest Texas State Teachers College, San Marcos, Texas, 1951, p. 44.

[16] The League, "Constitution," pp. 6-7; Weeks, op.cit., pp. 270-72.

[17] Weeks, op.cit., pp. 273-75.

[18] Ibid., pp. 260-61.

[19] The League, "Constitution," pp. 2-3.

CHAPTER III

THE AMERICAN G. I. FORUM: SECOND STAGE OF

MEXICAN-AMERICAN SOCIAL PARTICIPATION

Since its birth in 1929 The League of United Latin-American Citizens worked,
along with other lesser groups, to solve the problems of the Mexican-American population. This group of men and women, members of the Spanish-speaking ethnic group of
Texas, possessed a genuine interest in the acculturation of their people. Owing to the
lack of political organizations directly identifiable with the Spanish-speaking citizenry,
The League became recognized as the spokesman for this group of Americans. The
progress of this middle-class movement, however, did not satisfy the ambitions of the
more impatient members of the Mexican-American population of Texas.

The staggering political and social progress of the citizens of Mexican descent
became apparent with the coming of the Second World War, which involved many men
of Mexican background in all phases of military service, especially in the ranks of the
Army. For the first time these Texans had the opportunity to associate on equal terms
with men from all sections of the United States, giving the Spanish-speaking soldier the
occasion to identify with and prove his patriotism towards his country. This social
minglement was perhaps the first such opportunity Spanish-speaking Texans had ever
had.[1]

By the end of the struggle in 1945, the thousands of Mexican-American soldiers
who had seen combat duty had acquired a renewed sense of social obligation towards
their country and their people. Upon returning to their Texas homes many servicemen
were disillusioned to find that the political and social conditions of their ethnic group had
not changed despite the veterans' sacrifice of time and service in defense of the nation.

Many Anglo-Americans continued to regard the Americans of Mexican extraction as "Mexicans." The participation by members of this population in politics and civic functions was, as had been before the world struggle, slight.[2]

It became evident to many reform-conscious Texans that LULAC, in fostering the social, educational, and political betterment of Mexican-Americans, had progressed little in its endeavors.[3] In the late 1940's, as in the mid 1920's, a wave of enthusiasm engulfed the younger generation of Spanish-speaking veterans which made them desirous of a change, radical if need be, but one that would yield first-class citizenship. Of special interest to the would-be reformers was the political education of their people that would enable them to choose wisely representatives who understood well the needs and desires of the Spanish-speaking population. They sought organized unity in order to voice their grievances more effectively and to apply increasing pressure where needed.[4]

Many veterans of Mexican descent interested in social reform joined the ranks of The League of United Latin-American Citizens. Many others, however, regarded The League as passive and conservative in its approach to finding solutions to the needs and demands of the citizenry of Mexican descent. These reformers, as veterans of the Second World War and as citizens of the United States, sought equal rights and privileges for themselves, their families, and their people. They recognized that the most effective means to achieve this goal was through unified action.[5]

Among the returning young Mexican-American veterans who desired a better way of life for the entire Spanish-speaking population was Hector Perez Garcia, a physician from Corpus Christi. Garcia served from 1942 to 1946 as an infantry officer in the United States Army. He rose to the rank of major in the Medical Corps and received the decoration of the Bronze Star Medal with six battle stars.

Garcia, motivated by his desire to see the Spanish-speaking people enjoy the same standard of living as Texans of Anglo-American background, set out to find solutions to the many problems that perplexed his people. Being in the medical profession, he was in daily contact with the poverty and sickness so prevalent among many members of his community.[7]

On March 26, 1948, Garcia called together a small group of veterans of Mexican descent for the purpose of uniting into an organization, more effective than The League, designed to work towards improving the living conditions of the Mexican-American citizenry. These men named their newly-formed veterans' organization The American G.I. Forum of Texas and planned for productive expansion throughout the state. Within one year of their initial gathering, Forum leaders established local groups in most towns of South and Southwest Texas.[8]

Garcia and his fellow-forumeers became convinced that the solutions to many of their people's problems could be found in forceful political action while, at the same time, maintaining independence from any political faction, party, or individual. In setting the purposes of their organization, the founders called for the governmental education of the majority of the members of the Spanish-speaking population. The constitution of the American G.I. Forum, therefore, proclaimed the group's goals and purposes as follows:

> . . . [to] strive for the procurement for all veterans and their families, regardless of race, color, or creed, the equal privileges to which they are entitled under the laws of our country. . . . To foster the training and education of our citizens in order that a true and real democracy may exist in the lowest as well as the highest unit so that our loyalty to these principles may never be questioned.

> As loyal citizens . . . we sincerely believe that one of the principles of democracy is religious and political freedom for the individual and that all citizens are entitled to the right of equality in social and economic opportunities and that . . . we must advance understanding between the different nationalities.[9]

In accordance with these ideals, The American G.I. Forum, although a veterans' organization, unravelled its interests and activities to include the amelioration of all Spanish-speaking people. Its structure was designed to encompass as many people as possible. The founders designated certain areas of the state as districts under the direction of the State Board of Directors, the policy-making body of the organization. Each district, in turn, assumed organizational jurisdiction over the groups within its boundaries.[10]

Once organized, the members and leaders of The American G.I. Forum proceeded without delay to work towards the achievement of better social standards for their people. The Forum men and women hoped to accomplish what The League of United Latin-American Citizens left undone in improving race relations in Texas. The new civic group took a strong stand against segregating Spanish-speaking children in the public schools of the state. In a period of seven years, from 1948 to 1955, as a result of this avid interest in this field, G. I. Forum attorneys accomplished, through the federal courts, the integration of several school systems. [11]

Among the many examples was the Driscoll Independent School District case, where children of Mexican descent were segregated in the first two grades and where their attendance in these two grades was required for a period of four years. [12] After Gordon Green, superintendent of schools, refused to unite the Spanish-speaking and English-speaking children, Richard Casillas, Albert Pena, Jr., and James DeAnda, attorneys for the plaintiffs and members of The American G. I. Forum, appealed their grievance before James Winfred Edgar, Commissioner of the Texas Education Agency. The education agency magistrate, however, upheld Green's decision to keep Driscoll schools segregated. The Spanish-speaking attorneys then filed the case in United States District Court of the Southern District of Texas. The court's decision, delivered on January 11, 1957, overruled the Driscoll school officials and Commissioner Edgar, ordering the integration of the system since ". . . grouping of pupils on the basis of ancestry was arbitrary and unreasonable. . . ."[13] The successful conclusion of this and other legal actions encouraged officials from other schools to merge the two groups of students in the same classrooms without any legal action. [14]

The leaders of The American G. I. Forum became avidly interested in other areas of civil rights. Several members of the organization volunteered their legal services to solve cases dealing with violations of the equal rights of Mexican-Americans. One of the more celebrated legal actions, the outcome of which benefitted all Americans of Mexican descent, was that of Hernandez v. The State of Texas. [15]

The jury of Jackson County court convicted Pete Hernandez, a resident of Edna, Texas, for the murder of Joe Espinosa, a resident of the same community. The court judge assessed Hernandez a life sentence. Carlos C. Cadena and Gus Garcia, San

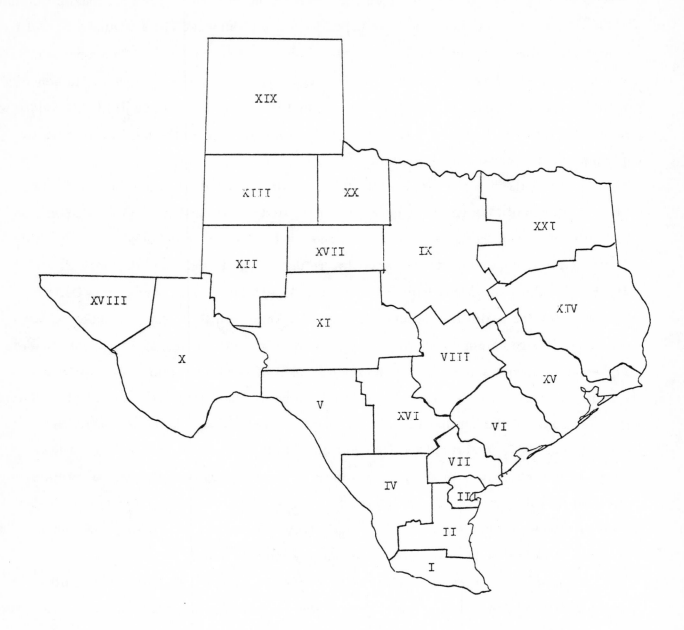

Fig. 1--This map illustrates the districts of The
American G.I. Forum of Texas.

Source: The American G.I. Forum of Texas, "The Constitution of The American G.I. Forum of Texas," McAllen, Texas,
1963, p. 12.

Antonio Attorneys defending Hernandez, appealed the case before the Texas Supreme Court of Criminal Appeals on the grounds that an all-Anglo-American jury convicted Hernandez, a citizen of Mexican descent. The state tribunal, the highest appellate court for criminal proceedings, upheld the decision, "since persons of Mexican-American descent are white. . . . Hernandez in being tried by an Anglo-American jury was tried by a jury of his peers."[16]

Cadena and Garcia then filed suit before the United States Supreme Court. In reversing the decision of the Texas court, Chief Justice Earl Warren held that since persons of Mexican descent had been systematically excluded from service as jury commissioners, grand jurors, and petit jurors, although qualified persons resided in that community, Hernandez had to be tried again. Chief Justice Warren, in delivering his decision, stated that

> Circumstances or chance may well dictate that no persons in a certain class will serve on a particular jury or during some particular period. But it taxes our credulity to say that mere chance resulted in there being no members of this class among the over six thousand jurors called in the past 25 years. The result bespeaks discrimination, whether or not it was a conscious decision on the part of any individual jury commissioner. The judgement of conviction must be reversed.[17]

While some leaders of The American G.I. Forum championed the causes of the Spanish-speaking citizenry in the courts, others set out to teach their people civic responsibility. These social reformers were aware that the average American of Mexican descent seldom enjoyed his voting privilege as a member of a democratic society. In consequence, in November of 1955, the veterans' organization launched one of the most vigorous poll tax payment campaigns ever seen in the history of the Mexican-Americans of Texas. Forumeers, with the cooperation of members of the American Federation of Labor and The Congress of Industrial Organizations, organized a group known as The Rio Grande Democratic Club for the purpose of executing the drive to induce people to pay their poll tax. This campaign, owing to its intensity, was confined to Texas's three southernmost counties--Cameron, Hidalgo, and Willacy.[18]

The Rio Grande Democratic Club, at the conclusion of its civic functions, pub-

lished a pamphlet entitled, "Texas Needs Four Million Voting Citizens," in which it re-
viewed its most significant accomplishments and made some recommendations as to how
the Mexican-American population could become more politically effective. The booklet
showed that in 1950 only 27 percent of qualified voters of Mexican descent paid their poll
tax. With these findings the members of the Rio Grande Democratic Club revealed the
apathy of Mexican-Americans throughout the state. As a result of the intensive campaign, the voting power of the Spanish-speaking citizenry shifted in 1954 from 43 percent
of its potential to 53 percent in the following year. [19]

The temporary existence of this civic club helped to alert the Spanish-speaking
citizenry of Cameron, Hidalgo, and Willacy counties of their voting privilege. Several
Rio Grande Valley newspapers, accustomed to the political inactivity of Mexican-Americans, attacked this move as "a union plot to take over the Valley," and accused the
members of the American G.I. Forum of "promoting class and racial warfare."[20] This
criticism, however, did not deter the leaders of the veterans' organization from pursuing
their intended purpose of alerting their people to political activity.[21]

The leaders of The American G.I. Forum continued in their effort to emphasize
the many facets of the plight of the Spanish-speaking citizens. Shortly after organizing
their group, these civic leaders began working for the elimination of the long-standing
"wetback" problem, which involved illegal entrants from Mexico into the United States
to work in the fields. These Mexican aliens became known as espaldas mojadas [wet-
backs] because the majority entered into the United States by swimming or wading
across the Rio Grande, the boundary which separates the two countries. These immigrants, for the most part representatives of the lower stratum of Mexican society, were
habitually ". . . humble, amenable, easily dominated and controlled, and [proved to]
accept exploitation with the fatalism characteristic of their class."[22]

During the 1930's and 1940's the number of wetbacks who came to Texas increased every year. By the early 1950's, however, their number soared to alarming
proportions.[23] These destitute aliens accepted jobs in the fields for meager wages with
which Mexican-American citizens, living and raising their families by American economic standards, could not compete. Texans of Mexican descent were left with the

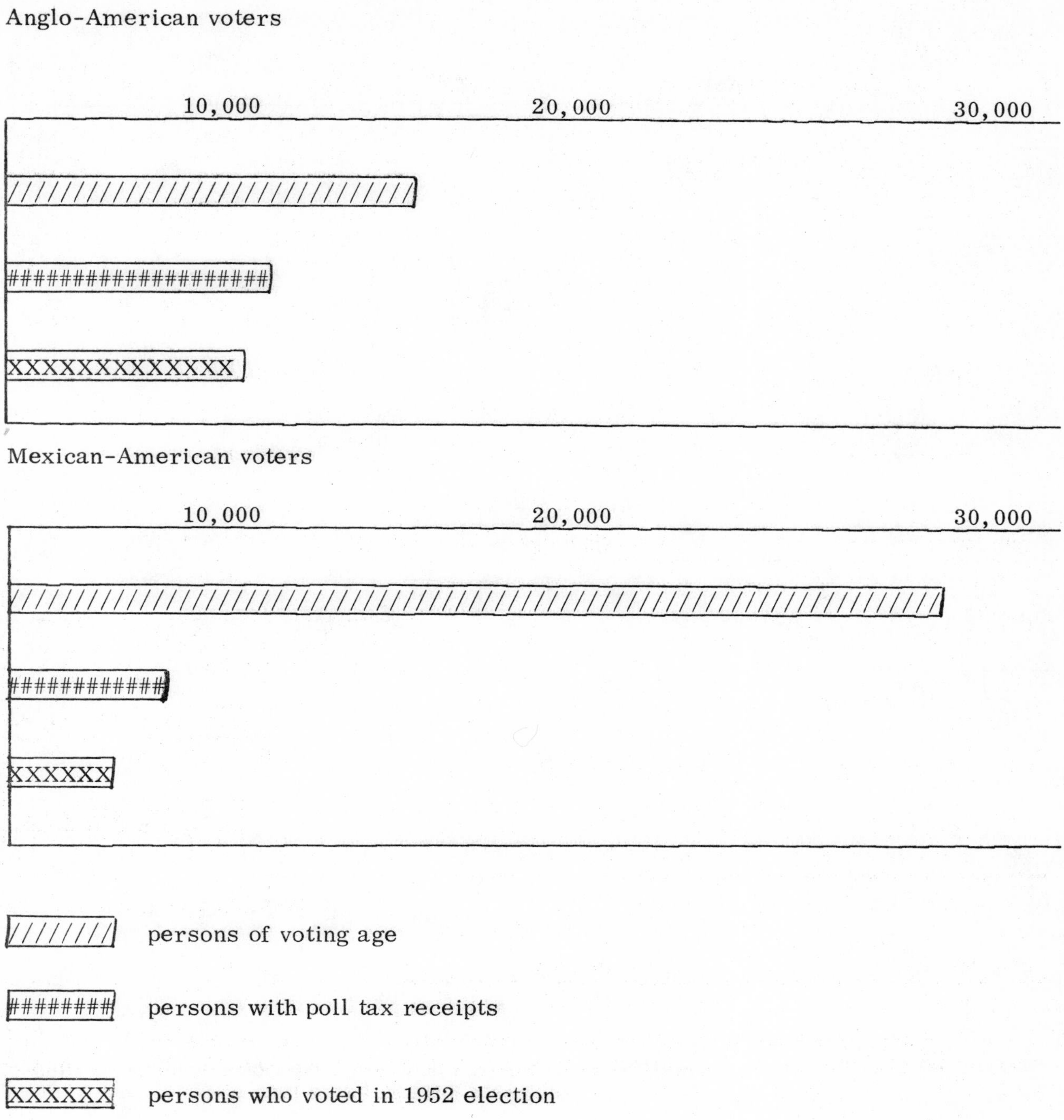

Anglo-American voters

	10,000	20,000	30,000

///////////////////////////////

####################

XXXXXXXXXXXX

Mexican-American voters

	10,000	20,000	30,000

//

############

XXXXXX

/////////	persons of voting age
########	persons with poll tax receipts
XXXXXX	persons who voted in 1952 election

FIGURE 2--A comparison of Anglo-American and Mexican-American voting participation in the 1952 gubernatorial election in Cameron, Hidalgo, and Willacy counties.

Source: Rio Grande Democratic Club, Texas Needs Four Million Voting Citizens McAllen, 1956, p. 2.

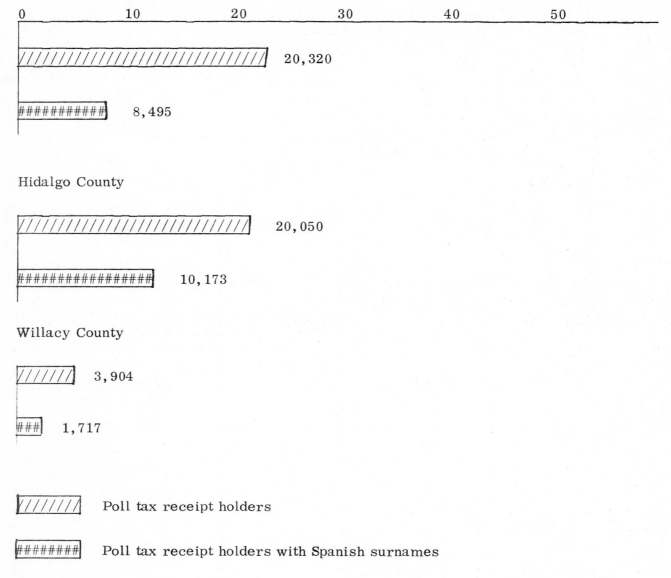

Cameron County

20,320

8,495

Hidalgo County

20,050

10,173

Willacy County

3,904

1,717

///////   Poll tax receipt holders

########   Poll tax receipt holders with Spanish surnames

FIGURE 3--A comparison of poll tax receipt holders with Spanish surnames to the total poll tax receipt holding population after the campaign of the Rio Grande Democratic Club in 1955 to induce Mexican-Americans to pay their poll tax.

Source: Rio Grande Democratic Club, <u>Texas Needs Four Million Voting Citizens</u> McAllen, 1956, pp. 6-9.

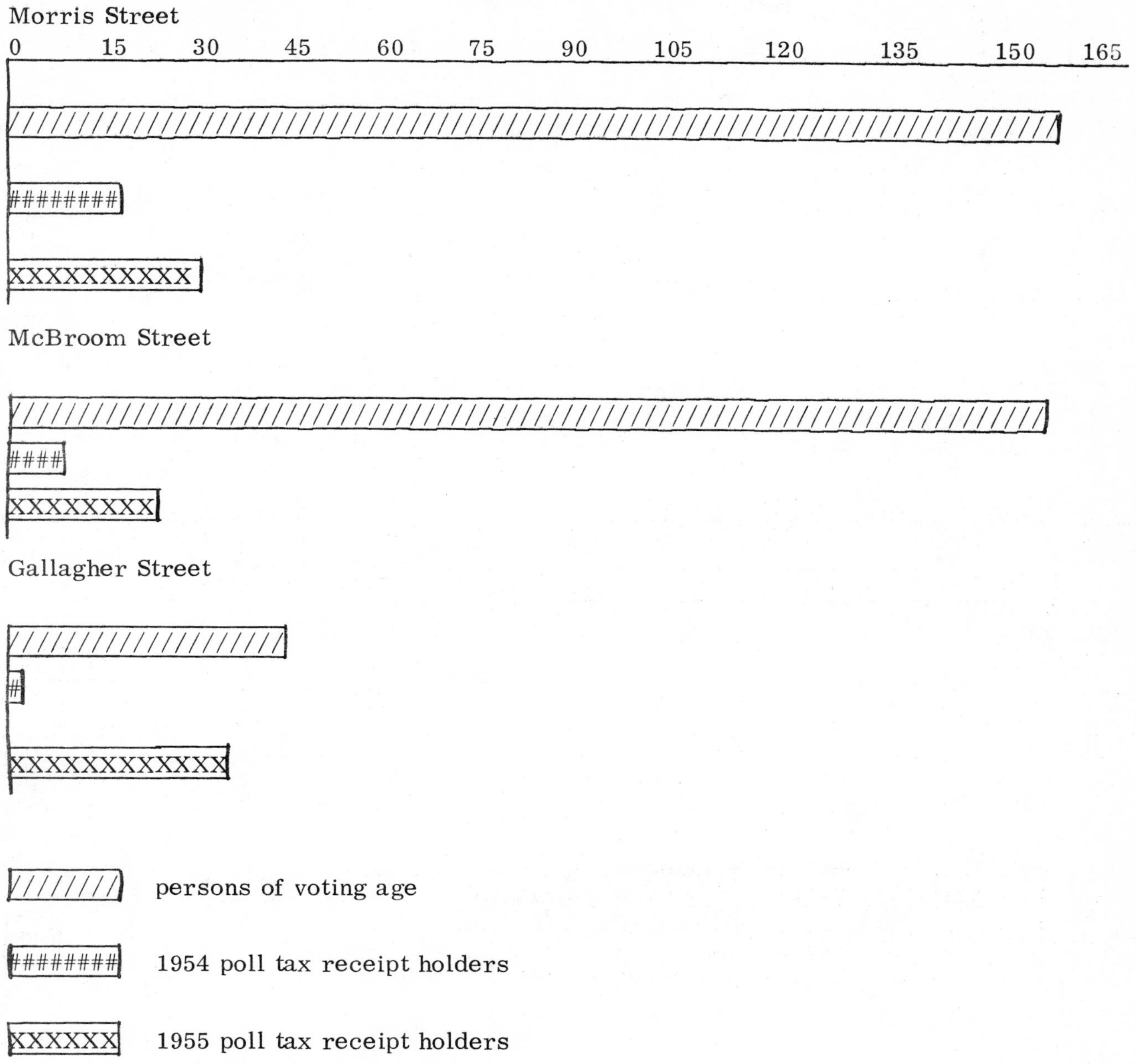

Morris Street

```
0    15   30   45   60   75   90   105  120  135  150  165
```

McBroom Street

Gallagher Street

/////// persons of voting age

######## 1954 poll tax receipt holders

XXXXXX 1955 poll tax receipt holders

FIGURE 4--The result of house to house campaign to encourage Spanish-speaking citizens to pay their poll tax in McAllen, Texas in 1956.

Source: Rio Grande Democratic Club, <u>Texas Needs Four Million Voting Citizens</u> McAllen, 1956, p. 16.

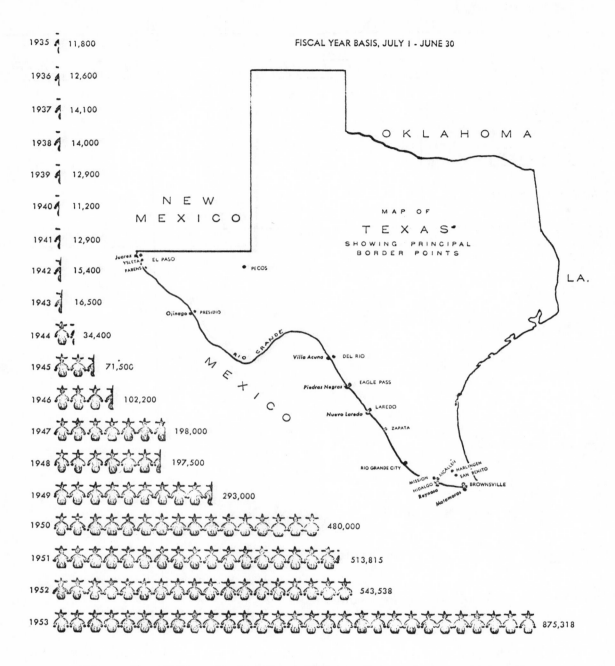

Fig. 5—Illegal immigration of Mexicans into Texas based on apprehensions made by the Border Patrol.

Source: The American G.I. Forum of Texas and Texas State Federation of Labor, <u>What Price Wetbacks?</u> (Austin, Texas, 1955), p. 31.

alternative of migrating with their families to other parts of Texas and to different states in search of better-paying jobs. [24]

The United States Border Patrol in Texas, charged with the responsibility of controlling the inrush of illegal entrants into the state, found it most difficult to police the entire 900-mile frontier from Brownsville to El Paso with a scant 491-man force. The leaders of The American G.I. Forum, well aware of this situation, wished to make the governmental agencies and legislators aware of the problem in the hope that favorable legislation would regulate the wetback traffic. [25]

The Mexican-American veterans' organization, aside from its own efforts, enlisted the cooperation of other interested groups and individuals in an attempt to bring the immigration situation to the attention of responsible agencies. The state conventions of the members of The American G.I. Forum produced strong resolutions calling for more effective control of the Texas-Mexican border. The leaders of the group then applied pressure upon government offices pertinent to the problem of immigration, such as the Department of Immigration and Naturalization Service, the United States Department of Justice, and Congress. [26]

The climax of this crusade came in 1953, when the American Federation of Labor and The American G.I. Forum combined their efforts to make a detailed study of the wetback problem in Texas. The organizations selected a two-man team, Edward Idar, Jr., of McAllen, a law student at the University of Texas, and Andrew C. McLellan, a Rio Grande City businessman, to survey the living conditions of the Mexican aliens in the state. The resulting research revealed the number of annual illegal Mexican entrants into the state and the circumstances under which they existed. [27]

In 1953 the sponsoring groups published the accumulated information in a pamphlet entitled, What Price Wetbacks?. With premeditated carefulness, the leaders of The American G.I. Forum and the American Federation of Labor distributed approximately 3,000 copies of the booklet to all interested agencies and public officials. As a result of these findings the United States Department of Immigration and Naturalization made a strenuous attempt to establish a tighter control along the Rio Grande border. As a consequence of the more careful surveillance, a decline in illegal entries became clearly evident.[28]

The success of The American G. I. Forum and the American Federation of Labor in influencing the control of illegal entry of Mexican labor into Texas was marred when a different form of immigration, braceros and commuters, replaced wetbackism. The bracero, a legally contracted laborer to work in the United States, entered the country under authorization by Public Law Seventy-Eight of the 82nd Congress, enacted in July, 1951. The American G.I. Forum promptly voiced its opposition to this program of contracted labor. Through its widely circulated report, What Price Wetbacks?, the veterans' organization argued that enough workers existed in Texas to warrant abolishment of Mexican labor. The authors of the pamphlet blamed the foreign low-wage earners for some of the economic ills of the Texans of Mexican descent.[29]

The commuter, a Mexican citizen holding a Resident's Crossing Card, had the privilege to shop, to visit, but not to work in the United States. These cardholders disregarded the law and commuted daily to accept low-paying jobs as maids, service-station attendants, and similar manual tasks. Because they maintained their homes in Mexico and lived by Mexican economic standards, the commuters could work for extremely low pay and still support their families located south of the border. In their opposition to this practice, organizations such as The American G.I. Forum and The League of United Latin-American Citizens met with little success. The problem continues.[30]

The American G.I. Forum, although a non-political group, cautioned its members to avoid endorsing "any one person or candidate or party for any public office," but urged them "to take an active interest in their government and in political action either as candidates or as individuals."[31] Accordingly, the group's membership individually participated in various poll tax paying campaigns and conducted classes as part of their program to overcome political apathy among their people. In addition, G.I. Forum members voiced their views about issues which affected the social progress of the Mexican-American citizen by forwarding pertinent letters to government officials and elected representatives of the people. Many of these views were given further dissemination through The American G.I. Forum Bulletin, the organization's monthly newspaper, with an approximate circulation of 10,000 copies.[32]

In 1954 the leaders of the Mexican-American civic group, in an attempt to impress upon the government officials the Spanish-speaking population's desire for equal representation in the governmental state offices, became involved in a political squabble with Texas Governor Allan Shivers, who failed to appoint Spanish-speaking persons to government posts. In his bid for renomination by the Democratic Party in the second primary election of August, 1954, Governor Shivers lost the support of Mexican-Americans, who, supported his opponent, Ralph Yarborough, a practicing attorney in Austin, Texas.[33] One month after this election, the victorious Shivers, apprehensive of the Mexican-Americans' resentment, placed two attorneys of Mexican descent in district judge posts. It then became obvious to many G.I. Forum leaders that Shivers, in making such appointments, made a deliberate attempt to recapture their support. Spokesmen for the veterans' group criticized the tactic as ". . . the first step to mend a fence that cost him [Shivers] thousands of straying Spanish-speaking votes."[34]

In 1958, leaders of The American G.I. Forum similarly criticized Governor Price Daniel for opposing minimum wage standards for agricultural workers. During its 1958 state convention the Mexican-American organization censured the governor in a resolution which stated:

> Whereas, . . . Governor Price Daniel asked the United States Department of Labor to revoke its regulation requiring that alien agricultural workers be paid a fifty-cent per hour minimum wage and has referred to said regulation as 'unfair' and,

> Whereas, said regulation, inadequate though it is, will to some extent improve the economic conditions of the American agricultural worker . . . and,

> Whereas, Governor Price Daniel, . . . deliberately disregarded the field worker's right to a decent wage and thereby grossly abused thousands upon thousands of Texans in order to satisfy the greed of a chosen few; . . . be it

> Resolved, that Governor Price Daniel be severely censured for requesting the United States Department of Labor to, in effect, plunge the agricultural worker further into economic slavery.[35]

The leaders of the veterans' league, in an effort to keep their people informed about governmental affairs, circulated pamphlets citing the voting records of the state's elected officials. This information, Forumeers hoped, enabled Mexican-American people to make an independent judgement as to which public officeholders kept with the interests of their ethnic group.[36]

The civic victories won by The American G.I. Forum attracted the attention of state politicians and enhanced the expansion of the organization throughout the Southwest. Leading spokesmen for the group traveled widely, appearing before government committees to present the grievances of the population of Mexican descent. Representative of this group was Richard M. Casillas, 1958 G.I. Forum state chairman, who spoke before the Texas State Tax Commission to voice the interests of his ethnic group. A sales tax increase was under consideration and Casillas, speaking for his organization, opposed any raise in taxes. He pointed out to the committee members that more taxes would impose a hardship upon the underpaid citizens, a great number of whom were Mexican-Americans.[37] In his attack on the state tax system, Casillas stated that,

> it is high time that our Legislature and public officials stop being the
> baby darlings of TMA [Texas Manufacturing Association] and the vested
> interests. It is time that they [the Legislators] . . . begin imposing taxes
> according to ability to pay. . . . A tax on corporate income is now im-
> perative and the answer to our State's financial ills.[38]

As a result of the various civic actions that the members and leaders of The American G. I. Forum undertook, the Mexican-American population gained some social and political stature throughout the state. Consequently, the organization continued to expand. Throughout the 1950's the veterans' league, during its state conventions, adopted resolutions pertinent to the goals and desires of Texans of Mexican descent. First, Forumeers resolved to establish an official American G.I. Forum office in Austin to keep in close contact with all state agencies, boards, officials, and the legislature. Such office, furthermore, could carry out more successfully lobbying for programs favorable to the Spanish-speaking population. Such office was established in 1958.[39]

A second resolution, aimed at the indifference of the public officials towards the needs of the Mexican-American population, stated:

> Whereas, Representatives and Senators in the Texas Legislature with constituencies made up of Spanish-speaking citizens either 'take a walk' or do not vote a great percentage of the time of issues affecting the welfare and progress of the Spanish-speaking citizenry, . . . be it

> Resolved, . . . that all such members of the Legislature to be urged to support actively issues affecting the welfare and progress of this minority group and . . . that henceforth Spanish-speaking voters will observe their [the legislators'] voting record and use this as a basis for individual action in future electoral contests.[40]

Such type of political action brought the organization of Spanish-speaking citizens to the attention of public officials, who began to recognize it as the spokesman for all Texans of Mexican descent. Politicians, consequently, began to seek the support of this organized league of veterans. Many persons of Mexican descent, no longer alien to Texas's government system, hoped for better representation for their people.

With the organizational groundwork laid by The American G.I. Forum and The League of United Latin-American Citizens, some Mexican-American political aspirants gained confidence to seek elective offices. These potential candidates, politically inexperienced, needed popular support to challenge the well-established Anglo-American governmental machines. The existing Mexican-American civic and social groups worked to provide the necessary backing to elect these interested Texans to public office where problems peculiar to this ethnic group could be solved.

FOOTNOTES

CHAPTER III

[1] Raul Morin, Among the Valiant: Mexican-Americans in WWII and Korea (Los Angeles, 1963), pp. 27-30; Carey McWilliams, North from Mexico: The Spanish-Speaking People of the United States (New York, 1948), p. 260.

[2] McWilliams, op.cit., pp. 260-61.

[3] Interview with Ed Idar, Jr., Attorney and Former Executive Secretary of the American G.I. Forum and The Political Association of Spanish-Speaking Associations, Austin, Texas, February 20, 1969.

[4] McWilliams, op.cit., p. 261; George I. Sanchez, "Cold Devastating Facts," a statement delivered to the Texas Legislature on April 15, 1963, mimeographed copy in possession of the author.

[5] The American G.I. Forum of Texas, "The American G.I. Forum and What It Stands For," pamphlet printed for The American G.I. Forum, McAllen, Texas, 1964, in the possession of the author.

[6] "Garcia, Hector Perez," Who's Who in the South and Southwest, Vol. X (Chicago, 1967), p. 340.

[7] Interview with Hector P. Garcia, M.D., founder of the American G.I. Forum, San Antonio, Texas, December 8, 1968.

[8] Ibid., Garcia stated that The American G.I. Forum was created primarily for the purpose of finding equal social and economic opportunities for veterans owing to this group's unquestionable citizenship status. Once veterans of Mexican descent found redress to their grievances the entire population would benefit.

[9] The American G.I. Forum of Texas, "The Constitution of The American G.I. Forum of Texas," unpublished document, McAllen, Texas, 1963, p. 1, located in the office of the Executive Secretary, The American G.I. Forum of Texas, San Antonio, Texas.

[10] Ibid., pp. 3-5. See figure 1.

[11] The American G.I. Forum Bulletin, April, 1955, p. 1.

[12] Hernandez et al. v. Driscoll Consolidated Independent School District, et al. 1384 (1957).

[13] Ibid.

[14] The American G.I. Forum Bulletin, April, 1955; Interview with Ed Idar, Jr., Attorney and former Executive Secretary of The American G.I. Forum of Texas and The Political Association of Spanish-speaking Organizations, Austin, Texas, February 20, 1969.

[15] Hernandez v. State of Texas, 406 U.S., 251 (1953).

[16] The American G.I. Forum Bulletin, June, 1954, pp. 1-5.

[17] Hernandez v. State of Texas, 406 U.S., 251(1953).

[18]The American G.I. Forum Bulletin, November-December, 1955, p. 1; Interview with Idar, February 20, 1969.

[19]Rio Grande Democratic Club, Texas Needs Four Million Voting Citizens (Mc Allen, Texas, 1956), p. 5. Figures 2, 3, and 4 illustrate some of the most significant findings of the Rio Grande Democratic Club.

[20]The American G.I. Forum Bulletin, November-December, 1955, pp. 10-11.

[21]Interview with Idar, February 20, 1969.

[22]The American G.I. Forum of Texas and the Texas State Federation of Labor, What Price Wetbacks? (Austin, Texas, 1953), p. 6.

[23]Figure 5 shows the rapid increase of illegal immigration into Texas from Mexico from the 1930's to the 1950's.

[24]The American G.I. Forum and American Federation of Labor, op.cit., p. 6.

[25]Interview with Idar, February 20, 1969.

[26]Ibid.

[27]Ibid.

[28]Ed Idar, Jr., State Executive Secretary of The American G.I. Forum of Texas to Gilbert C. Garcia, November 21, 1959, in possession of Gilbert C. Garcia, Fort Worth, Texas; Interview with Idar, February 20, 1969.

[29]The American G.I. Forum and the American Federation of Labor, op.cit., p.48.; Idar to Garcia, November 21, 1959.

[30]Idar to Garcia, November 21, 1959.

[31]The American G.I. Forum, "The American G.I. Forum," pp. 1-4.

[32]Ralph Casarez, 1967-68 State Executive Secretary of The American G.I. Forum of Texas, San Antonio, Texas, to the author, June 23, 1968.

[33]"Yarborough, Ralph," Who's Who in the South and Southwest, Vol. X (Chicago, 1967), p. 1060.

[34]The American G.I. Forum Bulletin, September, 1954, p. 4.

[35] The American G.I. Forum of Texas, "Censorship of Governor Price Daniel: Resolution adopted at the 1958 Convention on Saturday, July 5," San Antonio, Texas, July 5, 1958, located in the office of the Executive Secretary of The American G.I. Forum, San Antonio, Texas.

[36] Idar to Garcia, November 21, 1959.

[37] Richard M. Casillas, "Statement to Texas State Tax Study Commission," Austin, Texas, June, 1958, located in the office of the Executive Secretary of The American G.I. Forum, San Antonio, Texas.

[38] Ibid.

[39] The American G.I. Forum of Texas, "Conventions Resolutions, Resolution No. 2," Austin, Texas, August 28, 1953, p. 1, located in the office of the Executive Secretary of The American G.I. Forum, San Antonio, Texas; Interview with Gilbert C. Garcia, Former State Chairman of The American G.I. Forum of Texas, Fort Worth, Texas, July 10, 1964.

[40] Ibid., August 28, 1953, p. 4.

CHAPTER IV

EMERGENCE OF MEXICAN-AMERICAN POLITICIANS

Civic and cultural organizations, predominantly of Mexican-American membership, gradually awakened the Spanish-speaking population of Texas to political action. These groups--The League of United Latin-American Citizens and The American G.I. Forum--sought a better social and educational opportunity through a broad program of community activities for Texans of Mexican descent. As a prerequisite to more direct involvement in politics, Spanish-speaking leaders worked towards the elimination of social prejudices which plagued members of their ethnic group. These spokesmen urged their people to become political participants rather than disinterested bystanders. In addition, these community leaders hoped that qualified and capable political leaders, able to speak for the Mexican-American citizenry, would emerge from their masses. [1]

Before the mid-1950's many Texans of Mexican parentage who aspired to get elected to public office made an impressive but often futile attempt to fulfill their ambitions. Groups of citizens with partisan interests who wished to keep this population politically inactive, however, discouraged these upcoming politicians with offers of comfortable positions. As a result of such political tactics, lack of financial support, and little governmental sophistication, statesmen with Spanish surnames, aspiring to high elective offices in the state, seldom progressed up the governmental ladder. [2]

By the early 1950's a significant portion of Mexican-Americans had achieved some degree of political knowledge and had acquired the ambition to use it. This civic education marked the partial fulfillment of the goals previously set by the Spanish-speaking leaders of the various social clubs. The election of several Texans of Mexican descent to local and state elective offices served to demonstrate to active reformers of this ethnic group that the Spanish-speaking population had in fact progressed. While the list of Mexican-Americans who achieved some political prominance in Texas during the 1950's included several Spanish surnames, one who best represented the goals of the citizens of Mexican descent was Henry B. Gonzalez, United States Congressman from San Antonio.[3]

Born in 1916 in San Antonio, Gonzalez attended the local public schools and subsequently enrolled at Saint Mary's University, from which he received a law degree. After his graduation from law school, Gonzalez occupied various positions, including that of Chief Probation Officer for Bexar County. Elected in 1953 to the San Antonio city council, Gonzalez received economic support for his campaign from an economically dominant Anglo-American group ". . . long accustomed to practically hiring bright young Texas Mexicans as their legislative frontmen."[4]

The newly-elected city councilman, contrary to the desires of his political sponsors to stop orating about reform, made an unanticipated attempt to integrate city facilities in San Antonio. In 1956, after introducing the successful ordinance that finally removed all laws on segregation in the Alamo city, Gonzalez resigned from his position as city councilman to seek election to the state senate. Succeeding in his bid for this office, Gonzalez became the first Texan of Mexican descent to serve in the Texas senate in the twentieth century.[5]

Gonzalez, while a state senator, became an outspoken champion of equal rights for the Negro and Mexican-American populations. In 1957, for example, during the regular session of the Texas legislature, the freshman lawmaker filibustered for more than thirty-six hours on the senate floor to successfully block the passage of all but two of ten pro-segregation bills under consideration. One of the bills which became law provided for local elections on integration, while the second laid the groundwork for the assignment of school pupils in such a manner as to maintain segregation where desired. The lengthy talkathon in defense of integration, nevertheless, established the San Antonio senator as the liberal spokesman for Spanish-speaking and Negro Texans.[6]

In 1958 Gonzalez challenged the Democratic state organization and became an active candidate for governor of Texas against the incumbent Governor Price Daniel who was seeking a second term. The San Antonio legislator in his bid for the governorship conducted a vigorous campaign based on the proposition that "every man is equal before the law, regardless of race, creed, or color."[7]

Gonzalez, the first Spanish-speaking Texan to seek election to the highest electoral position in the state, officially opened his campaign on June 9, 1958, at La Villita, a restored Spanish village and the first building of the city of San Antonio.[8] Throughout his campaign, Gonzalez enjoyed the support of all state civic groups composed of Mexican-American citizens, whose leaders worked for the election of Gonzalez. In addition to the support of the voters of Mexican descent, Gonzalez attracted the Negro backing and the official endorsement of the National Association for the Advancement of Colored People of Texas.[9] Gonzalez, although with this support to boost his campaign, had little hope of winning the nomination of the Texas Democratic Party for the governorship but he became a contender ". . . to force Governor Daniel and the other candidates to make it clear where they stand."[10] To the surprise of many politicians Gonzalez polled enough votes to place second to Daniel, with W. Lee O'Daniel, a former Texas governor from Dallas, and Joe A. Irwin, a Dallas insurance man, trailing.[11]

Even though Gonzalez was defeated in his bid for the top state political office, his candidacy aroused for the first time in Texas history the enthusiasm of the Spanish-speaking citizenry and brought to the polls those voters needed to elect a liberal delegation in many parts of the state. The Mexican-Americans throughout Texas enthusiastically supported and worked for the candidacy of Gonzalez as ". . . the man that our race has been waiting for long years so that he may represent us adequately and honorably in the government of our state."[12]

The heavy voting in favor of Gonzalez, constituting an ill-organized coalition of liberal factions of the state, Mexican-Americans, Negroes, and labor, served as an indication to the state's conservative politicians of a potential liberal opposition with the Spanish-speaking population playing an important role. Even though the candidacy of a Texan of Mexican descent to defeat the political organization for the highest state office was, as Gonzalez put it, ". . . like fighting an eighty-ton tank with bricks," his campaign was a historic contribution to the political movement of the Mexican-American citizenry of Texas. In addition to being the first time in Texas history that a Spanish-speaking Texan challenged the conservative state government, Gonzalez's campaign demonstrated the dissipation of Mexican-American political apathy.[13]

Gonzalez, throughout his political career in Texas government as an advocate of equal rights, endeared himself to the liberally-oriented citizens of South Texas. His success in public office represented the success of the Mexican-American population. After his defeat for the governorship, the San Antonio lawmaker, continued to speak for his constituents in general and for the Spanish-speaking group in particular in the state government. On November 4, 1961, Gonzalez sought and won the election to the United States House of Representatives. Again, as in 1958, Gonzalez attracted much of the liberal support of the state. The candidate polled 53,138 votes against his opponent, John Goode, the Bexar County Republican chairman, who acquired a total of 42,707 votes. Gonzalez became the first Texan of Mexican-American background to be elected to the United States Congress.[14]

The newly-elected representative increased his status as one of the major moving political forces of the Mexican-American population of Texas. Recognized by his Spanish-speaking constituents as their leading spokesman in defense of their rights as American citizens, the San Antonian worked to advance the social and political conditions of his people. His philosophy concerning the civic involvement of Spanish-speaking Texans was that of moderation as opposed to the more militant alternatives offered by younger and more radical leaders of this ethnic group. Gonzalez advocated orderly and effective organization of his people to reach their desired political goals. This moderation in politics, Gonzalez claimed, would enable Mexican-American citizens "to build and participate" rather than "to get even or dominate. . . ."[15]

In advocating such organization of the Spanish-speaking Americans, Gonzalez favored a political group. Long active in the promotion of uniting his people, he recognized that ". . . it is certainly suicidal not to organize."[16] While co-chairman of a group designed to advance the election of John F. Kennedy and Lyndon B. Johnson during the 1960 Presidential election, Gonzalez foresaw the readiness of the Spanish-speaking population to launch a political organization capable of rallying the support of all the civic, social, and cultural groups of Mexican-Americans. A well-formed committee could present a unified front which would embrace beneficial progressive ideals. Such a group would not only exercise power through the ballot box or through the indirect support of a given political candidate, but through the active participation in sections of the state government by the majority of Texans of Mexican descent.[17]

FOOTNOTES
CHAPTER IV

[1]The American G.I. Forum, "The American G.I. Forum and What It Stands For," McAllen, Texas, July 23-24, 1964, located in the office of the Executive Secretary of The American G.I. Forum, San Antonio, Texas; Fort Worth Star Telegram, April 12, 1964, p. 10.

[2]Hart Stilwell, "Texas Rebel With a Cause," Coronet (August, 1958), p. 45.

[3]Ibid., pp. 43-47.

[4]Ibid., p. 45.

[5]Tommy Yett, editor, Members of the Legislature of the State of Texas from 1846 to 1939 (Austin, Texas, 1939), p. 130; Stillwell, op.cit., pp. 43-46.

[6]Stillwell, op.cit., p. 45.

[7]La Prensa, San Antonio, Texas, May 22, 1958, p. 16.

[8]Anonymous, A Twentieth Century History of Southwest Texas, (Chicago, 1907), pp. 11-16.

[9]Fort Worth Star Telegram, August 3, 1958, p. 16.

[10]Ibid.

[11]Ibid.

[12]Jim Presley, "Keg Beer and Gonzalez," The Texas Observer, September 5, 1958, p. 4.

[13]Labor: An International Weekly Newspaper, October 28, 1961; The Fort Worth Press, November 5, 1961, p. 10.

[14]Thomas B. Morgan, "The Texas Giant Awakens," Look (October 8, 1963), p. 71.

[15]Henry B. Gonzalez, Washington, D.C., to the author, December 13, 1968; The American G.I. Forum Bulletin, November, 1961, pp. 1-2.

[16]Morgan, op.cit., p. 71.

[17]The American G.I. Forum Bulletin, November, 1961, pp. 1-2.

CHAPTER V

POLITICAL ASSOCIATION OF SPANISH-SPEAKING

ORGANIZATIONS: FIRST MEXICAN-AMERICAN

POLITICAL GROUP

Henry B. Gonzalez, United States Congressman from San Antonio, while seeking the expansion of The American G.I. Forum, wrote, ". . . the American G.I. Forum is by far the only organization that augurs effective and cohesive effort in the direction of progress for this large and numerous group of Americans who up to now are devoid of effective and articulate organization. . . ."[1] Even though Gonzalez made direct reference to The American G.I. Forum, The League of United Latin-American Citizens, established in 1929, was also doing its share in accelerating the assimilation of the Spanish-speaking population of Texas and the Southwest to the American way of life. Gonzalez's statement, however, accurately pointed out that no effective political group existed which truly represented the interests of this ethnic segment of the American population.

Most Texas leaders of Mexican descent recognized the state government's neglect of their people. Such neglect was apparent in 1963 by the approximately 3,300 elective offices which existed in Texas, of which the Mexican-Americans held only thirty-one, and the 1,180 appointees to various state boards and commissions, of which only five persons had Spanish surnames.[2] A spokesman for this ethnic group had earlier expressed his concern when he said, "We have experienced difficulties in getting relief for the things that we are interested in from our state agencies and state officials . . . ."[3]

The small number of government officials representative of the Spanish-speaking population demonstrated to many ambitious Mexican-American citizens the impotence of their people as a political force in Texas. The Mexican-American leaders' foremost consideration, consequently, became the need to organize into a strong political group representative of the goals and aspirations of members of this ethnic group. The task of forming a political front was simplified by the accomplishments of The American G.I. Forum and The League of United Latin-American Citizens, the groups which for three decades had worked to advance the educational, economic, and social status of Texans of Mexican descent. By 1960, this process of civic education, even though incomplete, was at a stage which rendered this population ready to become politically involved.

The first opportunity for the Spanish-speaking leaders to organize came in 1960 when John F. Kennedy, United States Senator from Massachusetts, won the nomination of the Democratic party for the Presidency of the United States. The Texans of Mexican descent ". . . saw in the Democratic candidate a person whose demonstrated sympathy with and friendship for Spanish-speaking Americans entitled him to their support."[4] Many of the leaders of this group of Americans, cognizant of Kennedy's popularity with their people, formed an organization called "Viva Kennedy" to support the Democratic ticket.[5]

The idea for a Mexican-American movement in favor of Kennedy began in Wichita, Kansas, during the National Convention of The American G.I. Forum in August, 1960. Carlos McCormic of Arizona, a member of Kennedy's campaign staff and a long-time American G.I. Forum leader, and Hector P. Garcia of Texas, founder of the veterans' organization, gathered a group of Mexican-American leaders and established the plans for the launching of Viva Kennedy clubs throughout the states of the Southwest.[6]

In Texas this idea was put to practice when, after the formation of the first group in McAllen, Viva Kennedy clubs emerged throughout the state. The pro-Kennedy action in the Lone Star state, unlike any previous movement of the Mexican-American population, fostered the enthusiastic participation of this ethnic group in most political functions, promoting the election of the Democratic candidate. For the first time in the history of the Texans of Mexican descent the usual apathy shown towards politics disappeared. This population's important contribution to the election of the Democratic ticket to office wielded an influential civic precedence which became important in the formation of future political movements of the Spanish-speaking Americans. [7]

The Kennedy forces, while campaigning, took full advantage of the Mexican-American vote. They encouraged the full participation of the leaders of Viva Kennedy groups with promises that in case of a Democratic victory ". . . Mexican-Americans and other Hispano-Americans can be expected to be called upon to serve this country in ambassadorial and other posts. . . ."[8]

The design which became the symbol of the Mexican-American campaign in favor of the Massachusetts senator for President depicted Kennedy riding a Mexican burro into the White House. [9] This emblem became recognized throughout Texas as representative of a vigorous campaign waged by Americans of Mexican descent. The intensive voting of the Spanish-speaking population during the 1960 presidential election caused Newsweek magazine to write that "Mexican-Americans . . . helped like hell in Texas."[10]

The leaders of the Viva Kennedy movement, as a result of their participation in the presidential contest, gained the confidence to launch the first Mexican-American political organization in the history of Texans of Mexican ancestry. Such a group was to have a double purpose. First, it became a political front for the Spanish-speaking citizenry, and second, it served as a spokesman to seek the fullfillment of promises made by President-elect Kennedy. [11]

The Spanish-speaking leaders began transforming the Viva Kennedy club into a political organization when they formed an association called Mexican-Americans for Political Action (MAPA). Shortly after the initial organization of MAPA at Victoria, Texas, the founders decided, before further expansion, to change its name to Political Association of Spanish-speaking Organizations (PASO). [12] With the avowed purpose to function as the governmental representative for all civic and cultural Mexican-American leagues, the new group received the charge expressed in its constitutional preamble to "further the cause of good government and American democracy. . ." throughout the state. [13]

The leaders of the newly-formed political front expressed in a constitution that

Fig. 6--A facsimile of Senator Kennedy riding the Mexican burro into the Presidency as shown on the state Viva Kennedy Clubs membership cards. This design became the rallying cry for the Viva Kennedy Clubs.

Source: American G.I. Forum Bulletin, November-December, 1960, p. 1.

all persons interested in the plight of the Spanish-speaking population would unite and, through political action, find solutions to problems of an economic, educational, and cultural nature that afflicted the Mexican-American community. In addition, these leaders aimed to encourage direct involvement of their people in politics, hoping to achieve the election and appointment to local, state, and national office persons sympathetic to the goals of PASO. [14]

The leadership of the Political Association of Spanish-speaking Organizations, mostly former American G. I. Forum and LULAC leaders, lost little time in establishing its group as a political force in Texas. Soon after Kennedy assumed the Presidency in January, 1961, PASO spokesmen attacked his patronage policies as failing to involve prominent Spanish-speaking citizens in government posts despite their efforts in mobilizing the Mexican-American vote in support of the Democratic ticket in 1960. The PASO forces felt that the new Chief Executive had, by his failure to include members of their ethnic group in government positions, violated assurances made by his brother and campaign manager Robert Kennedy before the 1960 Democratic Convention, and by the President himself when he promised ". . . that prominent Spanish-speaking Americans would be appointed to major posts in formulating Latin-American policy."[15]

The new President of the United States, cognizant of his promises to the Mexican-American population, had named Hector P. Garcia, of Corpus Christi, one of the prime movers of PASO, as a member of the United States delegation which negotiated a mutual defense and aid treaty with the Federation of the West Indies. [16] In addition, Kennedy named Raymond L. Telles, Mayor of El Paso and long-time leader in Texas politics, as United States Ambassador to Costa Rica. [17] PASO leaders, however, felt that their contributions to the election of Kennedy to the presidency merited more appointments as political reward. [18]

In Texas the Political Association of Spanish-speaking Organizations was received with enthusiasm by liberal and conservative politicians alike. It soon became apparent to state governmental officials that such a group could play a decisive role in the approaching gubernatorial election of 1962. PASO leaders, determined to make an impressive beginning, actively sought to expand their organization throughout Texas to present a united front during the coming campaign. During one of the group's first gatherings in late 1961, its members selected Gilbert Garcia of Fort Worth, a long-time G.I. Forum state leader, as the official organizer for the new league. Garcia's responsibility was to form groups throughout Texas and to ". . . spark poll tax [paying] drives wherever possible."[19] During the same gathering, PASO spokesmen, in preparation for the 1962 state election, unanimously agreed that all members should remain politically neutral until the organization's endorsing committee interviewed each candidate and selected the one meriting their support "to avoid personality clashes and present a united front to everyone."[20]

The Texas gubernatorial election of 1962 was PASO's first test as a representative of Texans of Mexican descent. Many politicians became eager to witness the influence of the first political league of Spanish-speaking citizens in the state. Scott Sayers, 1962 Tarrant County Democratic chairman, for example, predicted an important PASO role during the election, when he said, ". . . look for the Latin-American bloc in Texas to have a big voice in Texas politics in May [1962]."[21]

Many aspirants to elective office approached individual leaders of the Mexican-American organization to solicit their support. One gubernatorial candidate, Texan Attorney General Will Wilson, addressed in a letter to a Spanish-speaking leader that,

> In addition to the many economic problems faced by . . . Texas citizens of Latin-American descent, I am becoming . . . aware every day of the total lack of representation by this group in the policy-making [sic] Boards and Departments over which the Governor has appointive powers. . . . I promise to you that I will take immediate action to change this if I am elected as your Governor.[22]

According to organizational policy, most PASO leaders remained uncommitted until the first state convention when candidates for state office wishing PASO's political backing were interviewed and evaluated. The February, 1962, gathering in San Antonio marked a good beginning for PASO on the state political scene. A candidate for lieutenant governor, Texas House of Representatives Speaker James Turman, called it "a new political era in Texas."[23]

During this meeting twenty candidates appeared before the Spanish-speaking group, each hoping to be endorsed. After campaign speeches were delivered, members of the Mexican-American organization questioned the public office seekers as to their views on representing the interests of PASO. As a result of this gathering it became evident to the Spanish-speaking leaders that most candidates for public office were sincerely interested in attracting the support of the Texas population of Mexican descent. Some political hopefuls made their appeals in a straightforward manner. A candidate for attorney general, for example, got up before the group and said, "I am here with my hat in my hand, asking your backing."[24]

The choices of the PASO endorsing committee, made during the San Antonio meeting after much discussion, surprised many Texans in political circles. Price Daniel, the incumbent governor who had been criticized repeatedly by Spanish-speaking leaders for his conservative policies, received the Association's endorsement for governor, while Don Yarborough, a Houston attorney, the most liberal candidate, lost the support he anticipated beforehand. The spokesmen for PASO endorsed Daniel because of their discontent with the liberal leadership. These Mexican-Americans, by backing a conservative over a liberal candidate, hoped to show the liberally-oriented politicians like Yarborough that the vote of the Spanish-speaking citizenry was not to be taken for granted.[25]

Other considerations, aside from the desire to castigate the liberal politicians, were considered by the Spanish-speaking group in selecting a candidate for governor of Texas. Questions were directed by a PASO committee at the candidates concerning inequities of Americans of Mexican descent. To this, Daniel modestly acknowledged that he ". . . did not know these things existed."[26] On the subject of Mexican-American representation on state boards and agencies, Daniel recognized his failure to give members of this ethnic group fair representation but showed himself willing to reverse the trend if elected again.[27]

The state Chief Executive, anxious to receive PASO's support, urged Texans of Mexican descent to apply for positions in the state Highway Patrol, where they would receive fair consideration. Of more importance to PASO leaders, Daniel promised to employ several members of their organization for his campaign.[28] Daniel, as governor of the state, could afford to make political promises to the membership of the Mexican-American league. Other candidates for governor, John Connally of Floresville and Secretary of the Navy in the Kennedy Administration, Don Yarborough, and Will Wilson, could not make such political promises to the members of the PASO endorsing committee.

While the selection of a gubernatorial candidate produced heated discussions within the membership of the association, candidates for lesser offices were endorsed with little difficulty. Gerard Secrest, state senator from Temple, received the backing for lieutenant governor. Secrest, a conservative, won PASO's endorsement because of his anti-segregation stand during the 1957 legislative session of the Texas senate. Other candidates selected by the Spanish-speaking group were Tom Reavley of Austin for attorney general and Woodrow Bean of El Paso for Congressman-at-Large.[29]

The endorsement of Daniel over Yarborough created some misunderstandings within the PASO leadership, as indicated by the close vote of fifty-one and one-half votes for Daniel while Yarborough received forty-one and one-half votes.[30] George Isadore Sanchez, University of Texas Professor of Education and a long time spokesman for Mexican-American equality, walked out of the San Antonio meeting in protest of the Daniel endorsement. Sanchez pointed out that the support for the governor violated the principles under which the organization was established--to seek representatives who were sympathetic to the problems of the Texans of Mexican descent. The university educator accused Daniel of ignoring the plight of his Spanish-speaking constituents and advised PASO leaders that "Principles rather than petty patronage must dictate our political choices."[31]

While patronage for Mexican-Americans was a criterion used by PASO leaders to select their candidates, the attitude of politicians towards the betterment of the Spanish-speaking population was foremost in the minds of the endorsing committee members. Harold Valderas, a Fort Worth attorney and delegate to the San Antonio PASO convention, summarized this attitude of the organization when he said, "Connally never asked us directly for our support."[32] Connally, therefore, by appearing indifferent towards the interests of this ethnic group lost the endorsement of the political league although he was favored by a large number of the delegates.[33]

Yarborough, the liberal candidate for governor, made an unfavorable impression upon the PASO assemblage and, as a result, alienated many of his supporters. "He told us," one delegate reported, "that he had 90 percent of the Latin vote in the bag, regardless of what PASO did."[34] Candidates such as Connally and Yarborough, furthermore, made few political promises to the Mexican-American group.[35]

An additional criterion leaders of the Political Association of Spanish-speaking Organizations considered important in singling out PASO endorsees was the candidates' chance of winning the election. These leaders believed that Yarborough, Connally, and Wilson had little chance of defeating Daniel. A PASO spokesman explained the membership's reasoning in endorsing candidates for state offices, saying:

> From 1950 to 1960 we supported candidates for Governor and lost every time. From past defeats we have learned that we must (1) have a candidate that offers a positive program with respect to our group, and (2) that also has a decent chance to win.[36]

The political Association of Spanish-speaking Organizations emerged from the 1962 gubernatorial campaign politically weaker. Don Yarborough predicted early in the campaign that PASO's endorsement would mean little to any politician, an assessment which became painfully evident throughout the contest for office. In San Antonio, for example, the Bexar County Democratic Coalition, a local group, supported and successfully delivered their share of the Mexican-American vote in favor of Yarborough despite PASO's urgings to side with Daniel.[37]

The failure of PASO's endorsed candidates to win the primary election was additional proof of the Spanish-speaking organization's failure to lead its people politically. This primary election was a setback for the first political front of the citizenry of Mexican descent.[38]

In May, 1962, after the primaries, the leaders of the Mexican-American group met in San Antonio to "discuss the problems of the organization as a result of the failure of the PASO endorsed candidates to make the runoffs."[39] Pessimism prevailed during this gathering. One leader noted that the developments during the campaign showed that the Mexican-American population was poorly equipped for political activity.

The most prevalent opinion among the political group's delegates, however, was that lack of unity within their ranks caused the organization's failure to induce Mexican-American citizens to rally behind PASO-SELECTED candidates.[40]

The failure of the political association to remain united during the campaign became even more evident in the November election when, although PASO had previously repudiated John Connally, the Floresville candidate carried most of the south Texas counties where the population of Mexican descent predominated. This political weakness of the Spanish-speaking activist group became increasingly significant as a feud between PASO leaders and Governor Connally developed. On August 26, 1962, after the primaries had eliminated Daniel from the contest for governor, the Spanish-speaking organization endorsed Connally, pending the candidate's acceptance of certain demands in return for PASO's support. Connally, however, assumed indifference towards this ethnic group's political backing and refused to compromise. PASO leaders, as a result of Connally's refusal to accede to their requests, withdrew their endorsement of the political candidate.[41]

The potentials and weaknesses of the Spanish-speaking population were revealed during the 1962 state gubernatorial election--PASO's political debut.[42] The Mexican-American organization began, in early 1961, by successfully rallying the support of most Texans of Mexican descent, but almost immediately its leaders fell to squabbling among themselves. Many PASO spokesmen, rather than compromise their political choice, ignored the organization's plea for unity. Throughout the 1962 campaign, therefore, the newly-organized league remained in constant turmoil despite the sincere efforts of the more sober leaders to keep the organization together.[43]

The young activist group initially represented the revolt of the youthful leaders of Mexican descent against the established political forces which dominated the state government. This revolt, however, suffered from lack of organization, funds, and unity, important factors in the realm of politics. The theoretical liberal coalition--made up of Mexican-Americans, Negroes, and labor--hoped for by many PASO leaders, was far from becoming a reality in 1962. The Mexican-American political group, instead, scrambled to assemble its badly divided forces and start over again with special emphasis on unison.[44]

The movement of the Spanish-speaking leaders to regroup their membership after the 1962 gubernatorial election continued with increased urgency in an effort to make their league an influential factor in state politics. Albert Pena, Jr., Bexar County Commissioner and PASO state chairman, admitted "that in its infancy PASO had ofen [sic] erred, but that it [PASO] was determined to help build a working coalition of all Texas liberals."[45] The leaders of the organization, with this goal in mind, sought the opportunity to prove the political potential of the Mexican-American population of Texas.

FOOTNOTES

CHAPTER V

[1] Henry B. Gonzalez, Texas State senator, Austin, Texas, to Stanley Valadez, Pittsburgh, Pa., September 7, 1958, in the possession of Gilbert C. Garcia, Fort Worth, Texas.

[2] Long Island Star-Journal, Long Island, New York, October 13, 1963, p. 17.

[3] Ed Idar, Jr., former Executive Secretary of The American G.I. Forum of Texas, McAllen, Texas, to H. T. Manuel, Austin, Texas, November 21, 1963, located in the office of the Executive Secretary of The American G.I. Forum, San Antonio, Texas.

[4] The American G.I. Forum Bulletin, November-December, 1960, p. 1.

[5] Ibid.; Interview with Ed Idar, Jr., former Executive Secretary of The American G.I. Forum of Texas, Austin, Texas, February 20, 1969.

[6] Interview with Idar, February 20, 1969.

[7] Ibid.

[8] The American G.I. Forum Bulletin, November-December, 1960, p. 1.

[9] See figure 6.

[10] Newsweek, November 21, 1960, p. 25.

[11] The American G.I. Forum Bulletin, November-December, 1960, pp. 1-4.

[12] Ed Idar, Jr., Texas State Executive Secretary of the Political Association of Spanish-speaking Organizations, to all members of the organization, February 8, 1961, located in the office of the Executive Secretary of PASO, San Antonio, Texas.

[13] The Political Association of Spanish-speaking Organizations, "Constitution and By-Laws of the Political Association of Spanish-speaking," McAllen, Texas, 1961, p. 1, located in the office of the Executive Secretary of PASO, San Antonio, Texas.

[14] Ibid., pp. 1-2.

[15] Valley Morning Star, Harlingen, Texas, June 28, 1961, p. 4.

[16] The American G.I. Forum Bulletin, March, 1961, p. 1.

[17] Foreign Service List (Washington, July, 1961), p. 16; Who's Who in America, Vol. XXXII (1962-63), p. 1731.

[18] The American G.I. Forum Bulletin, March, 1961, p. 1.

[19] The Political Association of Spanish-speaking Organizations, "Minutes of PASO Meeting," Laredo, Texas, December 27, 1961, located in the office of the Executive Secretary of PASO, San Antonio, Texas.

[20] Interview with Idar, February 20, 1969; PASO, "Minutes," December 27, 1961.

[21] Fort Worth Star Telegram, June 24, 1962, p. 7.

[22] Will Wilson, Attorney General of Texas, Austin, Texas, to Gilbert Garcia, Fort Worth, Texas, February 6, 1962, in possession of Gilbert C. Garcia, Fort Worth, Texas.

[23] The Texas Observer, February 16, 1962, p. 3.

[24] The Political Association of Spanish-speaking Organizations, "Minutes of PASO Convention," San Antonio, Texas, February 9-11, 1962, located in the office of the Executive Secretary of PASO, San Antonio, Texas.

[25] Interview with Idar, February 20, 1969.

[26] The Texas Observer, February 16, 1962, p. 1.

[27] PASO, "Minutes," February 9-11, 1962; Interview with Idar, February 20, 1969. Idar stated that Price Daniel, judging from the Governor's answers to questions of Mexican-American inequities, had been counseled beforehand as to the nature of

issues Spanish-speaking leaders would inquire about at the San Antonio meeting.

[28] PASO, "Minutes," February 9-11, 1962.

[29] Ibid.

[30] Ibid. Once the 1962 gubernatorial election was over, Sanchez aligned himself once again with PASO, owing to the more militant attitude of the group's leadership.

[31] PASO, "Minutes," February 9-11, 1962.

[32] Ed Idar, Jr., PASO State Executive Secretary, McAllen, Texas, to all PASO Officers, February 21, 1962; The Fort Worth Press, February 13, 1962, p. 4.

[33] Interview with Idar, February 20, 1969.

[34] The Fort Worth Press, February 13, 1962, p. 4.

[35] Interview with Gilbert Garcia, former PASO state organizer, Fort Worth, Texas, March 3, 1969.

[36] Ed Idar, Jr., State Executive Secretary of the Political Association of Spanish speaking Organizations, Austin, Texas, to "Fellow-Democrats," May 2, 1962, mimeographed letter in possession of the author.

[37] The San Antonio Light, March 11, 1962, p. 2b.

[38] Political Association of Spanish-speaking Organizations, "Minutes of PASO MEET," San Antonio, Texas, May 14, 1962, located in the office of the Executive Secretary of PASO, San Antonio, Texas.

[39] Ibid.

[40] Ibid.

[41] The Political Association of Spanish-speaking Organizations, "PASO Statewide Meeting, San Antonio, Gunter Hotel," San Antonio, Texas, no date, located in the office of the Executive Secretary of PASO, San Antonio, Texas; The San Antonio Light, October 8, 1962, p. 1; The Texas Observer, October 12, 1962, pp. 1-3.

[42] Interview with Idar, February 20, 1969. Idar stated that because of inter-rivalry and political differences PASO died in 1962 "the year when it started out to be the most effective."

[43] PASO, "Minutes," May 14, 1962.

[44] PASO, "Minutes," May 14, 1962; _The Texas Observer_, October 12, 1962, p. 4.

[45] _The Texas Observer,_ October 12, 1962, pp. 1-3.

CHAPTER VI

THE POLITICAL ASSOCIATION OF SPANISH-SPEAKING

ORGANIZATIONS AND THE CRYSTAL CITY ELECTION

Discontent within the ranks of the Political Association of Spanish-speaking Organizations which increased during the 1962 state elections marred the impressive beginnings of the group and weakened its political influence as a representative of Texans of Mexican descent. The leaders of PASO, in an effort to regroup their forces, sought the opportunity for action whereby the potential of the Mexican-American population could become unmistakably clear throughout the state. These leaders hoped, through an effective political campaign where PASO would emerge victorious, to prove the force of their organization. In this manner the group's initial failures would be overshadowed.

The opportunity for the Political Association of Spanish-speaking Organizations to prove its civic and political value appeared unexpectedly in Crystal City, Texas, "a sunbaked place, plagued by mosquitoes but proud of its self-imposed nickname 'The Spinach Capital of the World.'"[1] On April 2, 1963, Mexican-American citizens of this community gained, through the use of the ballot, city government control from a firmly-established city administration made up of Anglo-American residents, the group which had dominated politics since 1907, when Crystal City was established.[2]

Crystal City, a farming community of approximately 10,000 inhabitants located in the southwest part of the state in Zavala County, was, in many ways, a typical south Texas town where Spanish-speaking residents outnumbered their Anglo-American fellow citizens four to one. Such numerical superiority, however, had never obstructed the Anglo-Americans' ability to control the governmental, business, and agricultural interests of the community. Bruce H. Holsomback, a local banker, for example, held the Mayorship from 1929 until his defeat in 1963. [3]

The Crystal City Mexican-American political triumph, which climaxed with the election on April 2, 1963, of five town residents of Mexican descent to the city council, began as a local issue a year earlier. Juan Cornejo, local representative of the International Brotherhood of Teamsters of America, headed a three-hundred member labor union group. The union members comprised approximately 35 percent of the labor force of the California Packing Company, a vegetable cannery located on the outskirts of Crystal City. Cornejo and Andrew Dickens, a local retired oil field worker, launched a poll tax paying campaign among Mexican-American residents with the help of some labor union members. The management of the canning plant, however, discouraged all employees from participating in civic affairs. The employees obliged and the poll tax paying project was left unfinished. [4]

Lacking the power to challenge the directors of the cannery, the Teamsters representative sought outside assitance. Cornejo asked the leaders of the Political Association of Spanish-speaking Organizations in San Antonio, particularly Albert Fuentes, Jr., the group's state executive secretary, to assume control of the incomplete poll tax paying drive in the spinach capital. [5] PASO leaders, eager for political action, promptly accepted the challenge to match civic efficacy with the established administration in Crystal City. It became clear that PASO had chosen its pilot project. [6]

The leaders of the Spanish-speaking association moved swiftly. The Teamsters Union, with interests of further organization in south Texas, mobilized its own forces to help PASO with the project. [7] The PASO-Teamsters alliance, after completing the January, 1963, poll tax selling campaign, found that the Texans of Mexican descent had a plurality of poll tax receipts over the Anglo-American population. Of the 1,571 persons who paid the fee, 1,029 were residents of Mexican ancestry. Qualifying the majority of Spanish-speaking citizens to vote was a rare accomplishment for a community where, traditionally, this ethnic group had been lackadaisical about local elections. These results, therefore, exhilarated the already optimistic leaders of PASO. [8]

The original intention of PASO and Teamster leaders was to qualify the Mexican-

American citizens to vote. After the plurality of Spanish-speaking voters became clear, however, the original plan became an ambitious design to sponsor a slate of Mexican-American candidates for the city council. [9] The two major promoters of such scheme, PASO and Teamsters, selected dependable, although inexperienced, representatives to carry out the political drama in the farming community. PASO chose Martin Garcia of Kingsville, Texas, the organization's district director in the Corpus Christi area, to initiate the campaign. [10] Garcia, a part-time law student at Saint Mary's University, arrived at Crystal City in February, 1963. He was charged with the responsibility of creating a political group of the more interested Mexican-American residents and selecting five candidates for the April city council election to oppose the Anglo-American incumbents. [11]

The Teamsters' officials, at the suggestion of Fuentes, sent Carlos Moore to assist Garcia. Moore, a labor union director, was selected as technical adviser to the Spanish-speaking leaders, owing to his thorough knowledge of legal procedures dealing with election codes. In essence, he served as a political shield for the Mexican-American governmental novices. Moore's Anglo-American background and appearance allowed him to mingle freely with the leading citizens and city officials of the community who erroneously accepted him for an attorney. [12]

While Garcia and Moore worked in Crystal City, the state leaders of PASO and Teamsters supervised the affair from their headquarters in San Antonio. Fuentes directed the election campaign by calling in instructions to the civic workers in Crystal City and making several personal appearances. [13] Ray Shafer, Teamsters Union director and business agent, helped the campaign by making himself easily accessible for advice and assistance. [14]

Garcia and Moore, once present at the beleaguered town, immediately set out to unfold the plans for the city council election campaign which, throughout its duration, was marked by racial overtones. Their first move was to organize a group of Spanish-speaking citizens. On February 8, 1963, Garcia, Moore, and Cornejo conducted an organizational meeting attended by twenty-three local residents of Mexican descent. The assemblage formed the Citizens Committee for Better Government, and selected five of its members to be candidates for the local city council.[15]

The chosen candidates--Juan Cornejo, the local teamsters representative; Antonio Cardenas, a truck driver; Manuel Maldonado, a clerk in the town's Economart store; Mario Hernandez, a home salesman; and Reynaldo Mendoza, a photography shop operator--were representative of the majority of Mexican-American population of the community. They characterized the lack of educational attainment, the socio-economic plight, and the common background of the Spanish-speaking citizenry.[16]

The selection of uncultured and poorly-educated persons to run a political campaign and, if elected, to execute effective governmental control raised some questions among leaders of the opposition as well as some spokesmen for the Mexican-American population. Curtis Jackson, the Zavala County Attorney was quoted by The Texas Observer saying that "There is a very definite feeling that unless P.A.S.O. and Teamsters furnish the brains, that five-man team could not handle the job if they win."[17]

Garcia explained that he had approached better-educated citizens, but "The middle-class Latin-American doesn't have many grievances. There are few new frontiers for him."[18] On the question of little schooling of the candidates, Cornejo boldly replied that the candidates were educated in the ways of the majority of people whom they were seeking to represent. In addition to these justifications the candidates identified better with most of the Spanish-speaking citizenry and, therefore, could make a better case of ethnic differences.[19]

As the political contest progressed, campaign material poured into Crystal City from PASO headquarters in San Antonio. Posters arrived in sufficient amounts so that those destroyed by the opposition while displayed could be readily replaced.[20] Garcia, in a foresighted move, amassed the damaged campaign material and used its remains during rallys to show his people the opposition's tactics of destroying campaign material to stop the Mexican-American political efforts. In this manner the Mexican-Americans' anti-Anglo-American feelings were aroused and enhanced their desire to place their candidates in office. This strategy was characteristic of the many facets of the political campaign in Crystal City, which was based on racial differences and economic and social inequalities.[21]

Meanwhile, the Anglo-American city officials and their supporters, confident of their previously unchallenged positions as city administrators, regarded the movements of the Spanish-speaking population as insignificant. As election day approached, however, these leaders felt the impact of the vigorous Mexican-American campaign. They blamed outside influences for the actions of their fellow-residents. City Attorney Jay Taylor, quoted in The Texas Observer, summarized this feeling when he declared, "Certainly we're resentful of this union bunch coming in here and stirring up a bunch of rabble."[22]

The management of the canning plant, anti-unionist and supporters of the incumbent city officials, contributed to the attempt to thwart the Mexican-American campaign. In mid-March they dismissed two Spanish-speaking employees "for wearing campaign tags."[23] Teamsters union officials interceded on behalf of the discharged workers and reinstated them. Such action gave the Mexican-American employees some employment security and enhanced their participation in the political campaign.[24]

On election day, April 2, 1963, the area farmers, in an effort to keep the Mexican-American potential voters from the polls, offered field workers double wages. The leaders and members of the Citizen's Committee for Better Government counteracted by scouring the fields, encouraging their people to leave the fields and cast their ballot.[25]

To the surprise of almost everyone in the small town, the PASO-sponsored candidates were the five highest vote-getters and consequently the victors. The vote count revealed the following results: Maldonado 864, Cornejo 818, Cardenas 799, Hernandez 799, Mendoza 795, E. W. Ritchie 754, W. P. Brennan 717, B. H. Holsomback 716, J. C. Bookout 694, and S. G. Galvan 664. The last five candidates made up the incumbent City Council group.[26]

The Crystal City election, aside from being a triumph for the candidates, local farm workers, and Texans of Mexican descent, was, according to PASO leaders, a political victory for their organization. Fuentes claimed that on the day of election ". . . the Mexicans have learned all south Texans are equal."[27] Pena buttressed this opinion, saying that "Crystal City has opened the eyes of the sleeping giant [a term regularly applied to the Mexican-American population]."[28] Such exuberance on the part of the PASO leadership led to more political ventures, similar to the Crystal City contest, throughout south Texas.[29]

The Mexican-American governmental overturn in the southwest Texas community made a great impact upon many politicians throughout the state and the nation. This incident which, according to Look magazine, ". . . shivered the spines of many Anglo politicians in Texas," attracted wide attention owing to the unique manner in which it was accomplished--the combined efforts of the Political Association of Spanish-speaking Organizations and the Teamsters Union, two liberal forces.[30] This association successfully mobilized the traditionally apathetic population of Mexican descent to use its potential in grasping governmental control in the vegetable-raising community. Such a show of political force, if realized on the state level, posed a threat to the conservative establishments in many south Texas cities.[31]

The Crystal City event of 1963 had damaging consequences upon the Spanish-speaking organization as a political force in the state. This group, as a result of the election in the small community, split up into two distinct factions. During PASO's state convention of June, 1963, two months after the publicity ridden Crystal City episode, Hector P. Garcia, the prime mover of the national PASO organization, called for severence of PASO's relations with Teamsters. Garcia reminded the Mexican-American group that, "up to this time we have always done it [improvement of Mexican-American conditions] for ourselves," and in referring to the Teamsters participation in Crystal City, Garcia reminded his fellow-Texans that Spanish-speaking leaders "always looked with great displeasure on anyone from the outside telling us what is best for our people."[32]

Garcia's influence within the Spanish-speaking league led to a significant withdrawal of a portion of PASO's forces from the state organization. Pena and Fuentes, unlike Garcia, hailed their ties with the Teamsters as politically beneficial to the advancement of their people. "Anytime PASO thinks it can get the job done by itself," Fuentes declared, "it is dead."[33] Robert Sanchez, a McAllen attorney and influential political figure in the Rio Grande Valley, agreed with Fuentes when he added, "We have no permanent association with the Teamsters, but our needs are so great we will make a deal with the devil."[34]

PASO, criticized because of its affiliation with the Teamsters, was also condemned by its critics for its failure to choose well-educated and politically capable candidates to become city administrators. The weaknesses of these amateur officials of Mexican descent became evident in April, 1965, when an efficiently-organized "Anglo-Mexican-American" group, Citizens Association Serving All Americans (CASAA), posed five businessmen, three Mexican-Americans and two Anglo-Americans, as candidates for the city council and easily defeated the Cornejo administration.[35] Martin Garcia, 1963 organizer of the Mexican-American campaign, anticipated Cornejo's defeat when he said, "We taught them [the all-Mexican-American city council members] how to win an election, but we didn't teach them how to be politicians."[36]

The selection of almost-illiterate candidates, however, seemed inevitable and beyond the control of the Spanish-speaking group. The majority of affluent Spanish-speaking citizens refused to participate in such venture, fearing economic repercussions. The people of Mexican descent, therefore, turned to members of their group who best represented their interest.[37]

The Political Association of Spanish-speaking Organizations evidently failed, for the second time in its short life span, to establish itself as an influential political force in the state. Its participation in the gubernatorial election of 1962 manifested one of its greatest weaknesses--lack of unity among its leaders. The Crystal City election added to PASO's troubles. What started in 1962 as a failure to unite its elements became an organizational split following the political contest in the spinach capital when Hector Garcia, opposed to the PASO-Teamsters alliance, pursuaded his followers to desert the organization and continue working for the betterment of his people through civic organizations--The American G.I. Forum and The League of United Latin-American Citizens.[38]

PASO's 1964 state convention in Waco, more than three years after the association was organized, revealed the group's failure to create an impressive following among its people. This political gathering attracted only scant leadership from south Texas. According to Gilbert Garcia, a registered delegate, "no one west of Fort

Worth was present and many prominent leaders of the Mexican-Americans absented themselves, [and] the absence of mature leadership was clearly evident."[39] Even though a Waco newspaper report an attendance of 1,500 PASO delegates to the political assemblage, Garcia estimated the group at approximately 200.[40]

PASO, in its infancy, aimed to represent all the groups of Spanish-speaking membership in Texas. By 1964, three years after its beginnings, however, it evolved into a militant organization representative of only a small faction of Texans of Mexican descent. Its role in the formation of a liberal coalition capable of challenging the conservative forces throughout the state had little chance of becoming a reality, owing to its disparagement as a result of skepticism among Mexican-American leaders towards labor unionism. Gilbert Garcia, past state organizer for PASO, expressed his opinion that, "the teamsters union in Crystal City was interested in benefiting only Teamsters."[41] PASO's partnership with the Teamsters in Crystal City alienated many important leaders of the organization, such as Hector P. Garcia, who favored a moderate, go-it-alone approach to the social and governmental progress of his people.[42]

PASO, although badly damaged as a result of its first political victory in Texas, received the attention of the state's politicians. Immediately after the Crystal City historic election, when the voting potential of the Spanish-speaking citizenry of south Texas became apparent, PASO relished its highest point of achievement. This exhaltation, however, was short-lived. The withdrawal of the Garcia forces from PASO in June, 1963, left only disorganized remnants of the organization. The remaining leaders of the Political Association of Spanish-speaking Organizations worked to keep their league together but its significance as a political force in Texas became slight.

FOOTNOTES

CHAPTER VI

[1]The Dallas Morning News, May 7, 1963, p. 17.

[2]Political Association of Spanish-speaking Organizations, "What is PASO," mimeographed pamphlet, San Antonio, Texas, 1963, p. 1, in possession of the author; The Texas Observer, April 18, 1963, p. 3.

[3] Walter Prescott Webb, editor, The Handbook of Texas, Vol. I (Austin, Texas, 1952), p. 441; Thomas B. Morgan, "The Texas Giant Awakens," Look, (October 8, 1963), p. 72; The Texas Observer, April 18, 1963, p. 3; Interview with June Broadhurst, retired City Clerk of Crystal City, Crystal City, Texas, February 21, 1969.

[4] Interview with Juan Cornejo, former Crystal City Mayor, Crystal City, Texas, February 21, 1969. Cornejo stated that his sister and brother were among the employees dismissed from the cannery for participating in civic affairs; The Texas Observer, April 18, 1963, p. 3.

[5] Interview with Albert Fuentes, Jr., PASO state executive secretary, San Antonio, Texas, December 8, 1968; Interview with Cornejo, February 21, 1969. While Fuentes asserted that PASO went to Crystal City at the invitation of local citizens, Cornejo denied it.

[6] Interview with Fuentes, December 8, 1968.

[7] Interview with Gilbert Garcia, former state organizer for the Political Association of Spanish-speaking Organizations, Fort Worth, Texas, November 27, 1968; PASO, "What is PASO," pp. 2-4.

[8] Interview with Fuentes, December 8, 1968; The Texas Observer, April 18, 1963, p. 3. The Texas Observer cites 1,681 total poll tax receipt holders out of which 1,139 were residents with Spanish surnames.

[9] PASO, "What is PASO," p.2.

[10] Interview with Ray Shafer, Director of the International Brotherhood of Teamsters of America, San Antonio, Texas, February 20, 1969.

[11] Interview with Fuentes, December 8, 1968. Fuentes stated that the Teamsters Union provided the funds to pay Martin Garcia's tuition and expenses for one year in law school.

[12] Interview with Gilbert Garcia, former state organizer for the Political Association of Spanish-speaking Organizations, Fort Worth, Texas, April 20, 1967; Interview with Carlos Moore, field director for Teamsters Union, telephone conversation between principles in Washington, D.C. and Denton, Texas, February 8, 1969.

[13] Interview with Fuentes, December 8, 1968. Fuentes pointed out that Pena's activities in relation to the Crystal City campaign were limited but, as Chairman of PASO, sanctioned Fuentes's actions in the affair.

[14] Interview with Fuentes, December 8, 1968; Interview with Shafer, February

20, 1969; Interview with Cornejo, February 21, 1969. Fuentes stated that, contrary to popular belief, the Teamsters did not help the campaign with funds except the salaries of Garcia and Moore. Shafer stated that, "we helped with what little money we could." Cornejo stated that the Teamsters had provided them with campaign posters and "hand-cards."

[15]Interview with Cornejo, February 21, 1969; The Texas Observer, April 18, 1963, pp. 3-4.

[16]The Texas Observer, April 18, 1963, pp. 3-4; Interview with Cornejo, February 21, 1969. The five-member group averaged a seventh-grade education.

[17]The Texas Observer, April 18, 1963, p. 7.

[18]The Dallas Morning News, May 7, 1963, p. 17.

[19]Interview with Cornejo, February 21, 1969; Interview with Gilbert Garcia, November 27, 1968.

[20]Interview with Cornejo, February 21, 1969; Interview with Robert Canino, Chairman of PASO group in Austin, Texas, San Antonio, Texas, December 8, 1968. Canino attended a pre-election rally at Crystal City on April 1, 1963.

[21]The Dallas Morning News, May 7, 1963, p. 17.

[22]The Texas Observer, April 18, 1963, p.6.

[23]Interview with Fuentes, December 8, 1968.

[24]Fort Worth Star Telegram, October 12, 1963, p. 9.

[25]Interview with Fuentes, December 8, 1968; The Texas Observer, April 18, 1963, p. 8.

[26]The Texas Observer, April 18, 1963, p. 7.

[27]Interview with Fuentes, December 8, 1968.

[28]Interview with Albert Pena, Jr., Bexar County Commissioner and former PASO state Chairman, San Antonio, Texas, December 8, 1968.

[29]Interview with Fuentes, December 8, 1968. Fuentes stated that PASO had accomplished political victories in Mathis, San Marcos, Brownsville, Edinburg, McAllen, Lockhart, Victoria, Cuero, Goliad, Tohoka, and Ropesville, but that a different name was used every time to avoid controversy.

[30] Morgan, "The Texas Giant," pp. 71-72.

[31] Ibid.

[32] Interview with Hector P. Garcia, Founder of PASO and The American G.I. Forum, San Antonio, Texas, December 8, 1968. Garcia stated that PASO leaders could have been victorious in Crystal City without the help of labor, a probable conclusion.

[33] Interview with Fuentes, December 8, 1968.

[34] Morgan, op.cit., p. 71.

[35] The San Antonio Express, April 7, 1965, p. 2.

[36] The Dallas Morning News, May 7, 1963, p. 17.

[37] Interview with Fuentes, December 8, 1968.

[38] Interview with Hector P. Garcia, December 8, 1968.

[39] Interview with Gilbert Garcia, PASO state organizer and former state chairman of The American G.I. Forum, Fort Worth, Texas, July 10, 1964; Waco Tribune-Herald, February 16, 1964, p. 1.

[40] Waco Tribune-Herald, February 16, 1964, pp. 1-8; Interview with Gilbert Garcia, Fort Worth, Texas, July 10, 1964.

[41] Interview with Gilbert Garcia, November 27, 1968.

[42] Interview with Hector P. Garcia, December 8, 1968. Garcia also believed that The American G.I. Forum, the group which he founded, could enhance the progress of the Mexican-American population more effectively than PASO.

CHAPTER VII

CONCLUSION

The history of the Spanish-speaking population of Texas, as noted throughout this study, is synonymous with this group's struggle to overcome its social and economic subordination in a society where Anglo-American culture, language, and customs predominate. Mexican-American politics during this century have included several factors, namely, abolishment of prejudices against Americans of Mexican ancestry, improvement of educational facilities and opportunities, eradication of this group's social apathy, and elimination of any other inequities which plagued this ethnic group. Progress in these fields was, Mexican-American leaders believed, precursory to direct governmental participation of Texans of Mexican descent--as voters and candidates--in local, state, and national elections.

During the 1920's, affluent members of the Spanish-speaking citizenry, prompted by the social subordination of their people and by their aversion to be identified with a socially inferior population, grouped themselves to combat bigotry. This first major organization of Mexican-American membership, The League of United Latin-American Citizens organized in 1929, invited only the more advanced elements of this ethnic group to join in their fight. The League paved the way for more progressive groups to enhance this population's social status.

The advancement of the League was checked by the comprehensiveness of the social problems facing Texans of Mexican descent, the influx of Mexican immigrants, and the inherent conservatism of the organization's leadership. This civic group, nevertheless, continued to prod along making slow but significant progress.

The advent of the Second World War brought to light the persistent inequities which Mexican-Americans continued to endure in the United States. This disastrous world conflict, where Texans of Mexican descent fought by the side of their Anglo-American fellow-soldiers, served as an enlightenment to the Spanish-speaking fighting men. These young veterans returned to their homes with a strong desire of elevating the social standing of their people. Of special interest to the reform-minded Texans was the political education of the Mexican-American population. Such education, the returning veterans believed, was necessary before the voters of Mexican descent could choose wisely representatives who understood well their needs and desires. Herein lied a partial solution to the ills of this group of Americans.

The enlightened Texans, inspired by their strong ambition for egalitarianism, organized The American G.I. Forum. This group aimed to work towards the extinction of social barriers which had long prevented an understanding between the Mexican-American and Anglo-American populations. Ironically, this group of unified Spanish-speaking veterans, like the League of United Latin-American Citizens, sought action through non-political avenues. The American G.I. Forum leadership, nevertheless, unhesitantly applied pressure upon politicians for more effective representation of the Mexican-American people.[1]

The new group made significant strides towards the social improvement of the Texas citizenry of Mexican origin. Its membership, which numbered 10,000 in 1968, became instrumental in integrating public schools where children of Mexican descent received separate instruction and public facilities which barred Spanish-speaking Americans.[2] This organization became nationally recognized and became influential in government circles. To assert their effectiveness, Forum leaders established a central office in Washington, D.C. to represent the interests of Mexican-Americans throughout the Southwest.[3]

The progress of The American G.I. Forum and LULAC set the stage for Mexican-American individual quests for public office on all levels of government. During the 1950's many Texans of Mexican descent sought elective positions, particularly in the southern part of the state. Many candidates lost their bids for public office but many succeeded so that the decade from 1950 to 1960 became recognized as a period of significant political progress of the Spanish-speaking people.

Beginning with 1960 a drastic change in the social and political advancement of the Mexican-American population of Texas became apparent. During the 1960 Presidential campaign, this ethnic group overcame its traditional apathy towards governmental affairs and made an impressive contribution to the selection of the late John F. Kennedy to the Presidency of the United States. The innovation of a political group committed to represent the interests of the Mexican-American citizenry was assured as a consequence of such active political participation.

The newly-formed Political Association of Spanish-speaking Organizations, created in 1961, represented the beginnings of a Mexican-American bloodless revolution which replaced political torpor of members of this group with knowledge and changed their apathy to interested participation in civic affairs. This unified body, Spanish-speaking leaders anticipated, would solve the many problems which continued to plague their people. State public officials, long accustomed to a non-participating population of Mexican descent, looked upon PASO with suspicion and, sometimes, with antagonism, The realization of Mexican-American participation in government as an organization, proved to be more difficult than its founders anticipated.

PASO's failure to build a well-unified political front became evident during the 1962 gubernatorial election and the 1963 Mexican-American political takeover of Crystal City's administration. These ventures brought upon PASO attacks from its adversaries and caused a split in the ranks of the group from which it never recovered. The association, thereafter, decelerated its activities and undertook political campaigns under different names.[4] Thereafter, the organization played only minor roles in state politics.[5]

The Mexican-American population became politically divided into two factions --moderate and militant. PASO, the militant force, represented only a fraction of Spanish-speaking Texans with its stronghold in San Antonio. Its leaders, such as Albert Fuentes and Albert Pena, favored political takeovers by Americans of Mexican descent wherever their number warrants victory. In addition, politicians who, in the past, appeared indifferent towards the problems of the Spanish-speaking people became a target of PASO's criticism. These factors, however, were of little significance owing to the organization's failure to command a substantial following of Mexican-American people.

The moderate politicians, such as Hector P. Garcia and Henry B. Gonzalez, on the other hand, preferred gradual political involvement of their people, beginning with precinct, county, and up to state and national conventions. These leaders, furthermore, placed considerable importance in the educational achievements of their people as a prerequisite to political success.[6]

The activities of Mexican-American reformers and activist groups to bring about a speedy amelioration to social problems affecting this group of Texans have been multifaceted. Texans of Mexican descent, however, remain apathetic toward politics, social involvement, and education. They continue to be skeptical of political movements and civic organizations. This population's leaders, furthermore, still lack the know-how to exert political influence as a group. They tend, instead, to have several small organizations with similar goals but with different tactics.

The political progress of the population of Mexican descent depends on the ability of political and social reformers of this group, militant and moderate, to ignore personal differences and unite. These leaders, apparently, have not yet learned to strengthen their forces, through successful compromises among themselves, to offer a challenge to their political opponents and thereby play a decisive role.

The leadership that can exert the influence and organizational power to unite the Mexican-American population into an efficient political entity has not appeared. This ethnic group, therefore, continues to lack the political representation it needs. Civic leagues, through their efforts for social progress of the Spanish-speaking citizenry, awakened their people to the importance of active citizenship but failed to mold this population into an effective political front. PASO made a welcomed attempt to create such force but its organization soon waned owing to lack of unity and understanding among its own leaders.

FOOTNOTES

CHAPTER VII

[1]Interview with Hector P. Garcia, Founder of The American G.I. Forum and PASO, San Antonio, Texas, December 8, 1968.

[2]Ralph Casarez, 1968 State Executive Secretary of The American G.I. Forum of Texas, San Antonio, Texas, to the author, June 22, 1968.

[3]The American G.I. Forum of the United States, "D.C. Office Information," not dated, Washington, D.C.

[4]The Fort Worth Star Telegram, April 5, 1964, p. 1.

[5]Interview with Albert Fuentes, Jr., former State Executive Secretary of PASO, San Antonio, Texas, December 8, 1968; Henry B. Gonzalez, United States Congressman, Washington, D.C., to the author, December 13, 1968.

[6]Interview with Hector P. Garcia, December 8, 1968.

BIBLIOGRAPHY

Primary Sources

Unpublished Materials

Allee, A.Y., Carrizo Springs, Texas, to the author, February 6, 1969.

Casarez, Ralph, San Antonio, Texas, to the author, June 23, 1969.

Gonzalez, Henry B., Austin, Texas, to Stanley Valadez, Pittsburgh, Pennsylvania, September 7, 1958.

_____, Washington, D.C., to the author, December 13, 1968.

Idar, Ed., Jr., McAllen, Texas, to Gilbert Garcia, Fort Worth, Texas, November 21, 1959.

_____, McAllen, Texas, to Gilbert Garcia, Fort Worth, Texas, November 21, 1963.

_____, McAllen, Texas, to Texas members of The American G.I. Forum, February 8, 1961.

_____, McAllen, Texas, to State Officers of the Political Association of Spanish-speaking Organizations, February 21, 1962.

_____, Austin, Texas, to "Fellow-Democrats," May 2, 1962.

Political Association of Spanish-speaking Organizations, "Constitution and By-Laws of the Political Association of Spanish-speaking Organizations," unpublished document, McAllen, Texas, 1961.

_____, "Minutes of PASO Meeting," unpublished proceedings of PASO meeting, Laredo, Texas, December 27, 1961.

_____, "Minutes of PASO Convention," unpublished proceedings of PASO meeting, San Antonio, Texas, February 9-11, 1962.

_____, "Minutes of PASO MEET," unpublished proceedings of PASO meeting, San Antonio, Texas, May 14, 1962.

_____, "PASSO Statewide Meeting, San Antonio, Gunter Hotel," unpublished proceedings of PASO meeting, San Antonio, Texas, October, 1962.

The American G.I. Forum of Texas, "Censorship of Governor Price Daniel: Resolution adopted at the 1958 convention on Saturday, July 5," unpublished proceedings of The American G.I. Forum meeting, San Antonio, Texas, July, 1958.

_____, "Convention Resoltuions, Resolution No. 2," unpublished proceedings of The American G.I. Forum meeting, San Antonio, Texas, August, 1953.

_____, "The Constitution of The American G.I. Forum of Texas," unpublished Constitution of The American G.I. Forum, McAllen, Texas, 1963.

The League of United Latin-American Citizens, "The Constitution and By-Laws of the League of United Latin-American Citizens," unpublished Constitution, Austin, Texas, 1955.

Wilson, Will, Fort Worth, Texas, to Gilbert Garcia, Fort Worth, Texas, February 6, 1962.

Public Documents

Foreign Service List, Washington, Government Printing Office, 1961.

Hernandez et al. v. Driscoll Consolidated Independent School District, et al, 1384 (1957)

Hernandez v. State of Texas, 406 U.S. 251 (1953).

Inter-Agency Committee On Mexican-American Affairs, Cabinet Committee Hearings on Mexican-American Affairs, El Paso, Texas, Washington, Government Printing Office, 1968.

_____, The President's Remarks at the Installation of Commissioner Vicente T. Ximenes and a Cabinet Report on the Mexican-American Community, Washington, Government Printing Office, 1967.

President's Commission on Migratory Labor, Migratory Labor in American Agriculture, Washington, Government Printing Office, 1951.

Texas Legislature, Members of the Legislature of the State of Texas from 1846-1939, edited by Tommy Yett, Austin, Texas, 1939.

Texas State Senate, Journal of the Senate of Texas, 55th Congress, Austin, Texas, 1957.

United States Civil Service Commission, Study of Minority Group Employment in the Federal Government, Washington, Government Printing Office, 1965.

United States Civil Service Commission, Study of Minority Group Employment in the Federal Government, Washington, Government Printing Office, 1966.

United States Civil Service Commission, Study of Minority Group Employment in the Federal Government, Washington, Government Printing Office, 1967.

U. S. Congress, House of Representatives, Representative Gonzalez speaking about Poverty and Discrimination in the Southwest, 89th Cong., 2nd sess., May 12, 1966, Congressional Record, CXII, 10479-10483.

Reports

Rio Grande Democratic Club, Texas Needs Four Million Voting Citizens, Club Democrata del Rio Grande, McAllen, Texas, 1954.

Texas State American Federation of Labor and Congress of Industrial Organizations, 1962 Voting Record: 57th Legislature--87th Congress, Study it! Make Up Your Own Mind! Pay Your Poll Tax!, Austin, Texas, 1961.

The American G.I. Forum of Texas and the Texas State Federation of Labor, What Price Wetbacks?, Austin, Allied Press, 1955.

Encyclopedia

Moore, Walter, editor, Texas Almanac and State Industrial Guide, 1968-69, Dallas, The Dallas Morning News Incorporated, 1967.

Interviews

Interview with A. Y. Allee, Captain of the Texas Rangers, Carrizo Springs, Texas, February 21, 1969.

Interview with June Broadhurst, former City Clerk of Crystal City, Texas, Crystal City, Texas, February 21, 1969.

Interview with Robert Canino, former PASO chairman, Austin chapter, San Antonio, Texas, December 8, 1968.

Interview with Juan Cornejo, former Crystal City mayor, Crystal City, Texas, February 21, 1969.

Interview with Albert Fuentes, Jr., former State Executive Secretary of PASO, San Antonio, Texas, December 8, 1968.

Interview with Gilbert C. Garcia, former State Chairman of The American G.I. Forum of Texas and PASO State Organizer, Fort Worth, Texas, July 10, 1964; April 20, 1967, November 27, December 8, 1968, March 3, 1969.

Interview with Hector P. Garcia, M.D., founder of The American G.I. Forum and the Political Association of Spanish-speaking Organizations, San Antonio, Texas, December 8, 1968.

Interview with Ed Idar, Jr., former Executive Secretary of The American G.I. Forum and The Political Association of Spanish-speaking Organizations, Austin, Texas, February 20, 1969.

Interview with Carlos Moore, field representative for Teamsters Union, telephone conversation between principles in Washington, D.C., and Denton, Texas, February 8, 1969.

Interview with Albert Pena, Jr., Bexar County Commissioner and State Chairman of the Political Association of Spanish-speaking Organizations, San Antonio, Texas, December 8, 1968.

Interview with George I. Sanchez, Professor of Education at The University of Texas at Austin, Austin, Texas, June 24, 1968.

Interview with Ray Shafer, Area Representative for the Teamsters Union, San Antonio, Texas, February 21, 1969.

Secondary Works

Unpublished Materials

Bernal, Joe J., "History of School Segregation of the Mexican Americans," unpublished paper presented to the Department of Education, The University of Texas, Austin, Texas, 1968.

Casillas, Richard M., "Statement to Texas State Tax Study Commission," unpublished paper read before the Texas State Tax Study Commission, Austin, Texas, June, 1958.

Drury, Thomas J., D.D., "Statement by Bishop Drury," unpublished paper read before the State Board of Directors of The American G.I. Forum, San Angelo, Texas, June 21, 1963.

Garcia, Gilbert C., "Accomplishments of Mexican-Americans in Texas," unpublished paper submitted to the Department of Sociology, Texas Christian University, Fort Worth, Texas, 1958.

Political Association of Spanish-speaking Organizations, "What is PASO?," unpublished pamphlet, San Antonio, Texas, 1963.

Sanchez, George I., "Cold Devastating Facts," unpublished paper read before the Texas Legislature, Austin, Texas, April, 1963.

The American G.I. Forum of Texas, "The American G.I. Forum and What it Stands for," unpublished pamphlet, McAllen, Texas, 1964.

The American G.I. Forum of the United States, "D.C. Office Information," unpublished bulletin, Washington, D.C., no date.

Books

Anonymous, A Twentieth Century History of Southwest Texas, Chicago, The Lewis Publishing Company, 1907.

Bancroft, Hubert Howe, History of the North Mexican States and Texas, Vols. XV-XVI of The Works of Hubert Howe Bancroft, 39 vols., San Francisco: A. L. Bancroft and Company, 1884.

Fogel, Walter, Education and Incomes of Mexican-Americans in the Southwest, Division of Research Graduate School of Business Administration, University of California, Los Angeles, University of California Press, 1965.

Griffith, Beatrice, American Me, Boston, Houghton Mifflin Company, 1948.

Kibbe, Pauline R., Latin-Americans in Texas, Albuquerque: The University of New Mexico Press, 1946.

McWilliams, Carey, North From Mexico: The Spanish-speaking People of the United States, New York, J. B. Lippincott Company, 1948.

Morin, Raul, Among the Valiant: Mexican-Americans in WWII and Korea, Los Angeles, Borden Publishing Company, 1963.

Nance, Joseph Milton, After San Jacinto, The Texas-Mexican Frontier, 1836-1841, Austin, The University of Texas Press, 1963.

Vander Zanden, James W., American Minority Relations, New York, The Ronald Press Company, 1966.

Webb, Walter Prescott, editor, The Handbook of Texas, 2 vols., Austin, Texas, 1952.

Taylor, Paul Schuster, An American-Mexican Frontier, Nueces County Texas, Chapel Hill, North Carolina, The University of North Carolina, 1934.

Who's Who in America, Vol. XXXII, 1962-63.

Who's Who in the South and Southwest, Vol. X, 1967.

Articles

Morgan, Thomas B., "The Texas Giant Awakens," Look (October 8, 1963), 71-75.

Sanchez, George I., "The American of Mexican Descent," The Chicago Jewish Forum, XX (Winter, 1961-62), 120-24.

Stilwell, Hart, "Texas Rebel With a Cause," Coronet (August, 1958), 43-46.

Weeks, O. Douglas, "The League of United Latin-American Citizens: A Texas-Mexican Civic Organization," The Southwestern Political and Social Science Quarterly, X, (December, 1929), 257-78.

Newspapers

Fort Worth Star Telegram, August 3, 1958. June 24, 1962; October 12, 1963; April 5, 12, 1964.

Labor: An International Weekly Newspaper, October 28, 1961.

La Prensa, San Antonio, Texas, May 22, 1958.

LULAC News, El Paso, Texas, September, 1963.

The American G.I. Forum Bulletin, June, September, 1954; April, November-December 1955; November-December 1960; March, November 1961.

The Dallas Morning News, May 7, 1963.

The Fort Worth Press, November 5, 1961; February 13, 1962.

The Long Island Journal, Long Island, New York, October 13, 1963.

The San Antonio Express, April 7, 1965.

The San Antonio Light, March 11, October 8, 1962.

The Texas Observer, September 5, 1958; February 16, October 12, 1962; April 18, 1963; December 9, 1966; November 15, 1968.

The Valley Morning Star, Harlingen, Texas, June 28, 1961.

Waco Tribune-Herald, February 16, 1964.

Thesis

Garza, Edward D., "LULAC (League of United Latin-American Citizens)," unpublished Masters Thesis, Department of History, Southwest Texas State Teachers College, San Marcos, Texas, August, 1961.

DATE DUE	

GAYLORD   PRINTED IN U.S.A.